A PLANNED
AUXILIARY LANGUAGE

H · JACOB

A PLANNED
AUXILIARY LANGUAGE

*The fact which seems to blind us
with excess of evidence is that the
language obstacle is most
emphatically not a theory but a
condition.*

ALBERT LEON GUERARD

LONDON
DENNIS DOBSON LIMITED
MCMXLVII

FIRST PUBLISHED IN 1947 BY
DENNIS DOBSON LIMITED
29 GREAT QUEEN STREET
KINGSWAY . LONDON WC2

PM8008
J2

PRINTED IN GREAT BRITAIN
in 10-pt. *Plantin*
BY WHITEHILL (PRINTERS) LTD
BIRMINGHAM 19

61/R

AMONG THE IMPORTANT PROBLEMS of an international kind to be promoted now and after the war is that of a means of expression in a language easily learnt and used by all civilised peoples of the world. The International Morse Code of signals is an example of an accepted system of alphabetical and numerical communication, and what is wanted now is an auxiliary vehicle of language which will be as widely understood. The subject of an international auxiliary language has long been under discussion, but we seem to be no nearer agreement as to what this language should be than we were after the last war. In 1921, the British Association published a careful and comprehensive report on this subject, prepared by a committee representing humanistic as well as scientific interests, and in collaboration with the chief associations concerned with classical and modern languages as well as by consultation with a number of learned societies.

The British Association Committee was appointed after the International Research Council, at a meeting in Brussels in 1919, had taken up the question of an international auxiliary language and recommended the formation of an International Committee to enquire into the position and outlook of the subject. It was hoped that a central international organization would be formed, under the League of Nations, and be empowered to make the final selection of the international auxiliary language, if feasible, and to take measures to ensure for it the greatest possible degree of stability. Chairmen were appointed to represent national committees for France, Italy, Japan, and Belgium, and the chairman of the British Association Committee undertook to represent Great Britain on the Committee of the International Research Council.

The desirability of an International Auxiliary Language having been unanimously approved by the British Association Committee, attention was given to the advantages and disadvantages of the following three types:

(1) A dead language, for example, Latin;

(2) A national language, for example, English;

(3) An invented or artificial language, for example, Esperanto and Ido.

The claims for the use of each of these languages as an International Auxiliary Language were justly and concisely stated by their own specialists in the report of the Committee. After careful consideration of this and other evidence from high authorities at home and abroad, the Committee found itself unable to pronounce judgment in favour of a particular auxiliary language for international use. The conclusions reached may be expressed as follows:

(1) Latin is too difficult to serve as an International Auxiliary Language, and its advantages are out-weighed by its disadvantages.

(2) The great international languages of the past have all borne the marks of imperial prestige which prevented them from being welcomed by alien races. The adoption of any modern national language by the common consent of the chief nations is therefore unlikely, as it would confer undue advantages and excite jealousy, however impartial the promoters of the language might be.

(3) Invented languages constructed on scientific principles and adaptable to many diverse requirements are practical means of international communication. They are neutral and have advantages of simplicity not possessed by most national languages. What auxiliary language of this kind will meet with general approval remains to be decided by international agreement.

5

In the interest of international communication and the free expression of ideas, it is to be hoped that academic as well as scientific and commercial organizations will assist in the movement towards an agreed auxiliary language. A committee of the British Association on Post-War University Education has dealt with the subject recently in one of the sections of its report. It recommends that apart altogether from the academic study of language and literature, every university should require its students to be able to make themselves understood, by speech and writing, in an auxiliary international language. The Committee suggests that the Universities Bureau of the British Empire, in consultation with the American Bureau and the Association of University Professors and Lecturers of Allied Countries in Great Britain, could take up the subject very appropriately and prepare a report upon it. There is no better way of promoting interrelationships between the peoples of the world than that of a simple common language; and the construction of such an instrument should not be beyond the powers of responsible authorities—literary, scientific and commercial—working together in a common and needful purpose.

Sir Richard Gregory,
Bt., F.R.S.

Extract from an address to the Association of Special Libraries and Information Bureaux, reproduced by kind permission of Sir Richard Gregory, Bt., F.R.S.

Contents

PART I
GENERAL REVIEW OF THE CHIEF PLANNED LANGUAGE SYSTEMS
CHAPTER I

CHAPTER II

CHAPTER III

CHAPTER IV

CHAPTER V

PART II
STRUCTURAL PROBLEMS OF THE PLANNED LANGUAGE
CHAPTER VI

7

8

The Approaches to Artificial Language

By Harold E. Palmer, D.Litt.

Late Linguistic Adviser to the Japanese Department of Education and Director of the Institute for Research in English Teaching

IN ADDING THIS INTRODUCTORY note to the work of my colleague and friend H. Jacob on *International* Language, I am stressing the idea of *Artificial* Language. Let me state at the outset that I am using the term 'artificial' in its strict sense, *viz.*, created by the art of man, and not in the less accurate (and usual pejorative) sense of 'imitation', 'substitute'. I am using it in the sense that we live in artificial houses (as contrasted with the caverns that were the natural houses of our remote ancestors), wear artificial clothes (as contrasted with the furs, feathers, and shells of our remoter ancestors), use artificial tools (as contrasted with the natural implements of the eolithic age), that we ride in vehicles, all of which, from the wheelbarrow upwards, are artificial, and write with alphabets that are every whit as artificial as the most artificial language designed.

By many the whole question of artificial language has been prejudged by the use of the term 'artificial'. To say that a language is artificial is to condemn it. To accompany this term by a sneer is to attempt to prove *ipso facto* that an artificial language is undesirable, and perhaps impossible.

If, as is said, all roads lead to Rome, there are many roads that lead to the idea of the growing necessity for artificial, as contrasted with the natural or ethnical, languages.

Let us now examine some of these roads and those who travel along them.

I. THE ROAD OF UNIVERSAL BROTHERHOOD

Many of those who work for the cause of harmony and brotherhood between nations have said: 'The chief obstacle to universal peace, international entente and cooperation is the lack of a common language; the peoples cannot talk to each other, they cannot communicate one to another their benevolent intentions and so remove distrust and fear. Most natural languages are national languages which, from their very nature, can no more serve as an international language than can a National Anthem serve as an

International Anthem; therefore the International Language must be an artificial one.'

Quoting Raymond Frank Piper in *Language and World Unity*: 'The most extensively used of all constructed languages, Esperanto (*the one who hopes*), was deliberately designed as a step towards a religion of universal brotherhood. Its author, Dr L. L. Zamenhof (1859-1917), lived as a boy in Russian Poland amid bitterly clashing races, languages, and religions. Here Russians, Poles, Lithuanians Germans, and Jews misunderstood, feared, and jostled one another. The people of Europe in fact speak no less than one hundred and twenty languages, all mutually unintelligible; thirty-eight of these are used by more than a million persons. Then the brilliant idea occurred to young Zamenhof that the hostilities and hatreds among peoples might be relieved through intercourse in a common neutral language—neutral in the sense of being free from racial, national, religious, and other prejudices. Impelled by this stirring vision of peaceful concourse and eventual universal brotherhood, he proceeded to create a great synthetic language. Such a vehicle is painfully needed especially in the Polands and Alsace-Lorraines of the world. It is an indispensable condition of international understanding and harmony.'

2. THE ROAD OF THE DELEGATE

The work of international congresses is much impeded for want of a common language. Proceedings are held up at every moment by the intervention of interpreters who translate into one or more other languages what a speaker has said in his mother tongue, and committee work is hampered in a still greater degree. And what of the delegate who happens to be ignorant of any of the 'major languages' specified by the organizers of the congress?

'Then let English be the International Auxiliary Language, the Universal Second Language,' say some.

But the average delegate says: 'A very satisfactory solution of the problem for those whose language is English, for this means that these people will be for ever dispensed from the task of learning foreign languages, that each has the privilege of expressing himself in his mother-tongue—to the disadvantage of the others. It is not equitable that any one people should be privileged to so great an extent. Let the handicap be fair, and the language-learning task be the same for all. And what could be fairer than to ask from each the comparatively light task of mastering an artificial language?'

3. THE ROAD OF THE LANGUAGE-LEARNER

Natural languages, from their very nature, are exceedingly difficult to learn—or expressed alternatively, take a long time to learn. The reason for the difficulty—or length of time—is the cumulative effect of (1) many unfamiliar speech-sounds, (2) irregular spellings,

(3) vocabularies marked by redundancies, deficiencies and ambiguities, (4) irregular and illogical systems of derivation, (5) cumbrous grammatical and syntactical systems.

On the other hand modern artificial languages are marked in general by (1) a minimum of speech sounds, most of them common to all languages, (2) perfectly phonetic spellings, (3) adequate but simple vocabularies, (4) regular and logical systems of derivation, (5) the minimum of rules of grammar and syntax, all regular. For illustrations of these five facilities see the description of various artificial languages in the present volume.

It is, then, only to be expected that an artificial language can be mastered in from one quarter to one twentieth of the time needed for mastering any natural language—and such is indeed the case. The variation between this estimated 'one quarter' and 'one twentieth' depends on what is the learner's mother tongue and which of the artificial languages is the subject of study. The Chinese find any artificial language at least three quarters easier to learn than, say, English; while the English or Russians can master an artificial language in a twentieth of the time needed for learning Chinese. (In my opinion, backed by my experience in learning Esperanto and Ido, the latter is by far the easier language in that its 'five facilities' are greater than those of the former. However, the reader may judge for himself.)

The language-learner then says: 'If I am obliged to take the trouble to learn a foreign language, let it be a language that I can learn in the minimum of time—and that language is an artificial one.'

4. THE ROAD OF THE EDUCATIONIST

The saying 'what do they know of England who only England know?' may be aptly paralleled by 'what do they know of English who only English know?' Most educationists probably agree that the nature of the mother-tongue is best understood or appreciated when viewed from the outside. To view one's mother-tongue from the inside is comparable to propulsion *in vacuo*, to leverage without a fulcrum, or to estimating the value of an internal currency without comparing it with foreign currencies. This is one of the chief reasons for which the study of classical languages has been prescribed as a means of culture or of mental discipline. It is chiefly for this reason that Europeans study Latin or Classical Greek, that the pundits of India study Sanscrit and that the Japanese study Classical Chinese as part of their education. A knowledge of almost any foreign language reveals to us our own. Indeed the only English grammar generally known to the Englishman is that which has been gained as the reflection of the grammars of French or Latin.

Educationists hold it desirable that one should know something of the structure and nature of languages, just as it is considered desirable that the educated person should know something of the function and workings of mathematics or, in more modern time, the basic principles of sociology or citizenship.

Esperanto has been described as 'the layman's Latin' in that it contains, and so illustrates, the grammatical mechanisms of number, gender, case, agreement, etc.

And if it is true to say that those who know only English can know little of English, it is true to say that those who know only natural languages can know little of natural languages. Natural languages are partly rational and partly irrational. Much of natural language is an exemplification of logic and many of its thought categories conduce to orderly and clear thinking. The idiomatic element with which natural languages are shot through and through, clouds the un-idiomatic element and mars the whole. Charming as idioms may be as marking historical or literary vagaries, they are as out of place in systems of linguistic symbolism as would be inexact and fanciful symbols in shorthand or mathematics. Quaintness and oddity may enhance the beauty of a work of literature or art, but not the utility of an instrument of precision. Machines are no longer built as they were 50 years ago according to æsthetic patterns, and our railway carriages and omnibuses no longer recall the shape of the old stage-coach.

Architecture would never have found its true development if the architect of a house or temple had been forced to design it as the extension of the inhabited cavern or the sacred grotto or tree of primitive priesthood. The conception of orderly and pure language freed from its inherited bonds and blemishes could never have come into existence without the conception of artificial language—and the Road of the Educationist leads to this ideal conception.

5. THE ROAD OF THE SCIENTIST

Scientists the world over have common interests and aims. To a certain extent scientific terminology is international. The scientist says: 'All mathematical signs are of artificial creation and are there-fore understood universally. Our nomenclatures, including as they do the tens of thousands of zoological and botanical names, the names of mineral and chemical substances, etc., are made up of words abitrarily derived from various and mixed sources—and are universal. The great nucleus of our international language exists. Regularization is still needed; so that, for instance, the name of the liquid now variously termed *petrol*, *gasoline*, *essence*, *benzin*, etc. (all created words) shall have one and the same artificial name just as the substance *radium* has one and only one name, which is also of artificial creation. Let us proceed further, and do for vocabularies in general what has already been done for vocabulary in particular—and the result will be a complete artificial language.'

6. THE ROAD OF THE CODE-USER

Two business firms of two different countries, each ignorant of the other's language, wish to carry out a commercial transaction—to order goods, secure a credit, specify conditions. If the transaction is of a simple nature, neither party need use the language of the other, nor any national or natural language; they need no translator nor interpreter, for they have recourse to international commercial codes designed for this particular purpose. These codes consist of thousands of arbitrary groupings of letters, each of which corresponds to some specific word or sentence. These have been created by the compilers of codes, and are of purely artificial origin.

The business man says: 'Our artificial written language exists and works. Let now a code-deviser come along and compile a code of words that can be uttered as well as written—and the result will be a complete artificial language.'

The mariner says something very similar: 'The code of maritime signals was composed long ago; it is in daily use. An almost infinite number of combinations of flags will convey the meaning of almost any message we wish to send irrespective of national language. Quite recently British and Russian sailors were able to communicate with each other successfully in a situation where no other communication was possible. Let the groupings of this code of maritime signals be made pronounceable—surely an easy task for the expert—and the result will be a complete artificial language.'

7. THE ROAD OF THE ETYMOLOGIST

Those who have made a study of Comparative Etymology say: 'In analyzing the contents of dictionaries we find that at least 7,000 words are more or less common in spelling and meaning to the six chief European Languages: English, French, Spanish, Italian, German, and Russian, not to mention several minor languages. Most of these words have come into these languages not by the process of linguistic evolution from earlier forms but by deliberate acts of creation, borrowing, and adaption. We find that in certain types of texts one-third of the vocabulary is made up of these international words. Let this process of deliberate borrowing be extended to the remainder of the vocabulary—and the result will be a complete artificial language.'

8. THE ROAD OF THE WORD-COINERS

Jespersen has pointed out that a large proportion of our so-called natural languages is made up of the artificial element. And indeed we have only to glance at the pages of any fairly comprehensive dictionary to see how many words have come into existence, especially during the last two centuries, as a result of deliberation followed by decision.

A notable example is provided by modern Japanese. In 1858 the Japanese determined to adopt western civilization, science, and sociology. Their language provided very few of the words necessary to designate western institutions and activities. English-Japanese dictionaries of that period could give no Japanese words for, *e.g.*, *bank*, *telegraph*, or *gunboat*, but merely definitions of such words. Just as European scholars coin new words for new needs by combining Greek or Latin roots, so the Japanese scholars coined the new words needed by combining old Chinese roots. If we, needing a word for it, created the Greek compound *automatic telephone* (pronouncing it in the English fashion), so the Japanese coined the Chinese compound *self-move-lightning-speak-apparatus*, which they spelt and pronounced in Japanese fashion *ji-do-den-wa-ki*. But this is hardly intelligible to the Chinese who in the Mandarin dialect would pronounce it *tse-tung-t'ien-hwa-chi*.

Let us here stress the fact that few coined words are 'invented words' such as *kodak*. Coinages of this sort are extremely rare in modern artificial languages, indeed the 45 correlative words of Esperanto are probably the only examples. What the word-coiner does, is to take some existing word or root and to derive the new word from it.

When scientists first observed the power of attraction possessed by amber and other substances when rubbed with silk, they needed a new word to designate it. If they had identified it with the phenomena of thunder and lightning they might have called it, as do the Chinese, 'lightning spirit', or they could have invented a word to designate it, as did the Belgian chemist Van Helmont, who in the 17th century invented the word *gas*. What they did, however, was to take the Greek word *elektron*, meaning *amber*, replace the *on* by *icity*, and stretch the meaning to cover the new concept. Indeed, in more recent years, those who wished to coin a word to designate the ultimate unit of the atom took the *electr* of *electricity* and reappended the Greek syllable *on*, using it in the sense of *unit*, thus restoring the original Greek word but with a completely new meaning.

This is the method used by most compilers of artificial languages —indeed Ido, Occidental, and Novial contain no invented words at all. Therefore those whose business it is to coin words say: 'Artificial languages differ from natural languages only in so far as they are wholly artificial instead of being partly so.'

9. THE ROAD OF THE LEXICOGRAPHER

The chief duties of those who compile dictionaries are to collect data on (1) *Polysemia* (how many meanings may be expressed by one and the same word); (2) *Synonymity* (to what extent a given meaning may be expressed by two or more separate words); and (3) *Translation* (to what extent a given word in a given language may be translated by a given word in some other language).

Thus (1) according to the great Oxford Dictionary the word *at* has 36 separate meanings; (2) Roget's *Thesaurus* is a catalogue of concepts with all the ways in which they may be expressed; and (3) cross references in a bilingual dictionary show us that in comparing English and French:

one sense of *take* = *conduire*, and that
another sense of *conduire* = *drive*, and that
another sense of *drive* = *chasser*, and that
another sense of *chasser* = *hunt*, and that
another sense of *hunt* = *look*, and that
another sense of *look* = *regarder*, and so on.

Hence the need is felt for some organized system by which units of signification (semantemes) may be identified and listed. The 1,000 numbered 'categories' of Roget's *Thesaurus* constitute but a step in this direction, for as this classification is based on English words, it is no instrument for a general semantic survey. Semantemes must be mapped out, as are the 'isoglosses' of dialectology, in the form of contiguous areas. (Indeed some years ago I was able to construct a few maps of this sort, and that for the preposition *for* took three months.)

The lexicographer (or, more properly, the 'semantician') says therefore: 'Finding no common measure of speech-sounds in the letters of national alphabets, the phonetician, disregarding all traditional orthographies, has drawn up a general comprehensive alphabet in which one sign represents one and only one speech-sound, and one speech-sound is represented by one and only one sign. Similarly, finding no common measure of semantemes in natural languages, we must draw up an artificial vocabulary in which one word represents one and only one semanteme and one semanteme is represented by one and only one word. For this some artificial language is needed, and experiments have shown that such an artificial language is possible.'

10. THE ROAD OF THE PHILOSOPHERS

Pascal, Descartes, Leibniz, Wilkins, and other philosophers and logicians of the 17th century said much the same thing as the lexicographers of the present century, but with a different aim in view. Compilers of dictionaries have in mind students of languages—particularly foreign languages, whereas the philosophers are looking to a more perfect instrument of thought than are natural languages, with their redundancies, deficiencies, and antiquities. Wilkins, indeed, went further than his contemporaries in that he drew up the outline of a philosopher's language of this sort. It is as if the philosophers said: 'Let us find for each concept a word which will symbolize that concept and no other—and the result will be a complete artificial language.'

Thus we note the existence of different roads each with its travellers proceeding in the directions that interest them. Each of the groups of travellers may be unaware of the existence of the other roads or may be indifferent to the needs and aspirations of the other groups. Yet either the roads lead to the same end or their existence proves that the end, *viz.*, Artificial Language, is a reality.

The author of this book describes the various forms in which this end has been conceived, and deals with the subject under the broader heading of Auxiliary International Language.

Introduction

MUCH RESEARCH AND EXPERIMENTAL work has been undertaken during the last fifty years in the field of planned language. The object in writing this book was to collect the data and to provide a basis for discussion. The book was designed on the model of the standard work on international language *Histoire de la Langue Universelle* and its supplement *Les Nouvelles Langues Internationales* by Louis Couturat and Léopold Leau (Hachette, Paris 1907) bringing it up-to-date and dividing the subject into three distinct parts, (1) a brief history and description as well as a short grammar of the five chief systems of demonstrated usefulness, (2) a discussion of the theoretical aspects and their possible solution and, (3) reports on the efforts to utilize a planned auxiliary language for scientific nomenclatures and international communication.

As far as possible all systems have been treated in a uniform manner, giving a synopsis of their history, grammar, their principles of derivation and the affixes used, the methods of vocabulary selection, comparative texts, and finally a concise commentary representing the author's views. Some theoretical aspects call for special attention in the final formulation of a workable planned language; their implications have been discussed in Part II though it was not always possible to treat them without reference to other relevant problems. In Part III the practical attempts to arrive at a solution have been reported as far as they are known today; some of the technical data have had to be restated in order to present the problem of technical terminology in its proper perspective and setting. The book is therefore a work of reference rather than a report on interlinguistic development.

In the past it has been difficult to make comparative studies of the constructed systems from the limited material available, now mostly out of print. It is hoped that the following chapters be regarded as a basis for information which has not before been available except through the information of interested groups and societies.

The book is not intended to advocate any particular system or basic solution, but has been written, rather, as an analysis of planned

17

language systems which have proved their usefulness in speech and writing, thus qualifying as a basis for further research and examination. It would be idle to expect that any one system evolved over the last fifty years is able to solve all demands of modern science or to answer fully the needs of modern society, and much exploratory work will still be needed to define, for example, the function and signification of affixes and the relation of certain principles to the ease of learning the planned auxiliary language.

While the subject of a planned language has not yet been accorded academic status, it is left to the individual and to interested groups to obtain the information on the various proposals from the limited number of books available on the subject; the reader is urged to make as extensive a use as possible of the books mentioned in the bibliography.

For advice and criticism received I wish to thank Mr M. C. Butler, Mr A. E. Brighten, Harold E. Palmer, D.Litt., Mr A. W. S. Raxworthy, Mr Gilbert H. Richardson, as well as my wife for the revision of the MS and the encouragement received. I also wish to express my thanks to Dr S. Auerbach, Mr Robert S. W. Pollard, and Mr Gilbert H. Richardson for the loan of manuals, grammars, dictionaries, and reports.

On the Function of a Planned Language

THE ENQUIRY INTO THE function of a planned auxiliary language can best be divided into two parts, (1) what are the minimum requirements which any modern means of communication wil have to fulfil and, (2) what are the principles of planning that language to meet these requirements.

An international auxiliary means of communication must answer to the needs of the vast scientific and social life as it exists today, as well as being adaptable to any demands which might be made upon it in the future. The language, or code, or system of communication, must be able to express and to define simply, clearly, and precisely, all scientific and social transactions in speech and writing. It must, further, allow of constant adaptation to new fields of scientific and social activity.

If it is agreed that these demands are the minimum required, let us then examine which particular form the language, or code, or system of communication, should take. In order to examine the fitness for purpose of any proposed means of communication, I have selected three simple texts appertaining to the scientific, social, and economic life of civilized society; any system which can render these quotations in speech and writing will be considered fit for further examination, any system which falls short of rendering satisfactorily these quotations cannot be considered as fit for further enquiry as an international means of communication or a basis for the creation of a planned auxiliary language.

Electro-magnetic waves. Wide range of vibrations or wave-motions not requiring any known material medium for their propagation; at one time supposed to be propagated through a hypothetical 'ether'. Travel with a velocity of 300,000 kilometres (186,000 miles) per second. In order of increasing wave-length, the best known are gramma rays, X-rays, ultra-violet rays, visible light rays, infra-red (heat) rays, wireless or Hertzian waves.

(From *A Dictionary of Science*, Uvarov; Penguin.)

Scope of Social Security. The term 'social security' is used here to denote the securing of an income to take the place of earnings when they are interrupted by unemployment, sickness, or accident, to provide for retirement through age, to provide against loss of support by the death of another person, and to meet exceptional expenditures, such as those connected with birth, death, and marriage. Primarily social security means security of income up to a minimum, but the provision of an income should be associated with treatment designed to bring the interruption of earnings to an end as soon as possible.

(From *Social Insurance and Allied Services*, report by Sir William Beveridge; H.M. Stationery Office.)

Draft Customs Nomenclatures. Articles composed of several materials and not specially classified as such shall follow the classification appertaining to the material of that part which gives the article its predominating character in respect of appearance and use. In applying this provision to composite articles, component materials which are present only in a negligible amount, and which do not essentially affect the nature or character of the goods, shall not be taken into account.

(From *Draft Customs Nomenclature*, League of Nations, Economic Committee.)

To render any one or all of these statements in an auxiliary means of communication, we require nothing less than a complete and autonomous language, ethnic or constructed. To be fully adequate, the language must possess a high degree of precision which can be attained by assigning to each element one invariable meaning, *i.e.*, each element is monosignificant, a principle often referred to in subsequent chapters. A qualification is needed however, for no language—with however extensive a vocabulary—has so far achieved absolute monosignificance. Attempts have been made, in the form of codes, in which each term denotes one invariable object or has one invariable function. This practice is carried out for various sciences as well as for predetermined signals and codes for civil and military purposes. For a complete language, based on the customs and practices of our day, we will have to apply the discoveries of modern linguistics to attain a practicable compromise. A word or word element gains its precise signification only in its proper context, the full sentence, or even paragraph, or book. The principle of monosignificance is therefore understood to apply to the smallest but complete unit of thought, the sentence. Without that limitation the vocabulary would be far too large for practical purposes; with it the principle becomes at once reasonable and possible of achievement.

Opinions differ widely on whether it is preferable to choose an existing ethnic language for the functions of an international means of communication, or an artificially constructed one. The reasons for either solution are well known, but as this book has been written with the intention of finding the best basis for a planned constructed language, it seems fair to summarize briefly the linguistic arguments for such a choice.

The European languages have a more or less common grammatical structure. Tradition and culture have, over hundreds of years, contributed to evolve this common basis which can be the only possible one for a planned auxiliary language. It is the European root material, its elements, and its grammatical structure which provide the language builder with the basis for a precise, a simple, and an economic language. This evolution of ethnic languages has been a very gradual process of improvement and simplification consciously influenced by experts in other fields of science. It owes today more to the rapid development of science than to the genius of the men of letters. New terms and grammatical elements are created or defined to serve the purposes of new phenomena, and as new processes become public property, a corresponding growth in scientific nomenclatures is part of the essential development. Thus the constructed element in language plays today a far greater part than in the past and is bound to develop further. Quite apart from this increase in scientific terminology, considered simplifications in spelling and structure have been introduced by the French Academy, as well as by the Spanish and German authorities. Today language is no longer the product of nature alone, but the more deliberate result of the human mind, shaping and forming it to suit the growing needs of our civilization.

The argument that a constructed language is artificial applies today both to constructed and in large degree to ethnic languages, though the ethnic languages have an emotional appeal which no artificial language can ever hope to surpass. In scientific notation the ethnic language shows artificial tendencies while in the choice of vocabulary and grammatical elements the artificial language has much in common with European languages. There does exist, however, one important difference between the two as far as future fitness for purpose is concerned. The deliberate development of every ethnic language is dependent on its existent grammatical structure and on a vocabulary whose terms may have several meanings. It must be entirely *a posteriori*. A constructed language, on the other hand, can be planned according to principles which are chosen and selected to suit the purposes for which the language is designed. The planning of its structure may be *a priori* even though its elements are based on the known root material of the European languages.

There is much that is constructed in ethnic languages which has become, through association of ideas, part of our daily language. We use many makeshift terms which we no longer feel to be invented [*wire/less* is used to describe a complicated system of wave-lengths and is extended to mean broadcasting; once the term acquires a conventional signification, it can rarely be used to describe other activities carried out 'without wires']. The constructed language can be precise where natural languages are vague; the constructed language can be regular where the natural tongue is irregular [where English employs a number of negative prefixes as in *in/definite, il/logical, un/natural, ir/responsible, dis/regard, non/conformist*, etc., the planned language uses only one regular negative prefix.].

The second part of our enquiry relates to the principles of planning the auxiliary language. As this is the subject of the book it may suffice to give a brief summary. The term *international auxiliary language* or alternatively *planned auxiliary language* is used throughout the book in one sense only, to describe an autonomous means of communication able to express freely all thought, implying a fully developed system of grammar and a complete vocabulary. Such a language is to be a neutral means of universal communication which will in no way interfere with the national culture or the political structure of any community. It cannot become the instrument of national policy as it does not give privileges to any one nation at the expense of another. It might and is designed to be, in time, part of the educational equipment of every person of school-leaving age.

OTHER SUGGESTED SOLUTIONS

On the average, secondary school education devotes from four to six lessons weekly to the study of one or several foreign languages. Language lessons are given to pupils between the ages of 10 and 16 years or longer. Over a period of six years, the energy expended is about 1,200 lessons after deducting vacational periods. After such continuous study the student does not, generally, possess a command of the language or languages studied. Results vary according to the method of teaching employed and according to the general knowledge which he or she possesses at the beginning of the course. It is recognized today that, to acquire proficiency in the language, further study and practical experience in the country is desirable.

Bilinguism. Professor Allison Peers suggests a universal bilingual education in which English and Spanish should be the international currency (*Spectator*, June 19, 1942). English should be taught as a second language to Spanish-speaking peoples, and Spanish to the English-speaking peoples. Both languages should be taught to people who have different mother tongues. To facilitate this teaching he envisages a simplified form of both English and Spanish. He does not make it clear whether the simplified form refers to spelling, grammar, or vocabulary. His proposal would make one of two selected languages the common possession of all.

In putting this proposal forward Professor Peers makes, in fact, two distinct suggestions, (1) to teach two selected languages which, in time, shall become the common languages of the world and, (2) to reform and simplify both languages in a manner not specified by him.

To what extent does the proposal of Professor Peers conform to the 'minimum requirements'? We know that to learn an ethnic language demands a greater expense of energy than to learn a simple constructed one. To teach two ethnic languages would double this effort. If Professor Peers envisages simplifying one or both languages by means of a limited vocabulary, the result would be a language or languages which would not fulfil the 'minimum requirements' of an auxiliary means of communication for our society. If he thinks of grammatical reform he might meet very serious opposition, and if he wishes to introduce phonetic spelling he would meet with many objections without obtaining a language or languages which would be as easy as a constructed one. Both English and Spanish possess an adequate vocabulary but this vocabulary is not and cannot be made completely monosignificant according to the principles described above.

The proposal leads back to former conditions when one or several foreign languages were taught in some schools with the result that the student, after a study lasting several years, was unable to use his knowledge freely in speech and writing.

A Sign Language. In *Nature* (January 16, 1943) Sir Richard Paget published a proposal which was originally put forward by Professor Daniel Jones nearly twenty years ago.

Sir Richard Paget says that the sign language suggested as a means of international communication would be one in which every sign is the equivalent of a spoken word which is pantomimically related to the meaning it bears (like the Red Indian sign language). He enumerates seven distinct advantages for a systematic sign language:

1. That every sign will appear natural to all nationalities alike.

2. That—as experience has shown—the individual signs will be easily and quickly learnt and remembered.

3. That the symbolism—being essentially pantomimic—will be more direct than that of any spoken or invented language.

4. That the language will lend itself especially to use by children and the rising generation—as a form of play—and will give them at the same time a datum line from which to judge and compare the spoken languages.

5. That the sign language will be at once simpler, more concise, and more unambiguous than any spoken language—owing to the much greater versatility and precision of the human hands as compared with the human organs of articulation (lips, tongue, etc.).

6. That the sign language will be very easy to teach—on a world scale—by means of educational films and television, and that it will be free from all difficulties of pronunciation.

7. That there is already available a vocabulary of just under two thousand words, which any interested student of average intelligence might expect to acquire within a month. A longer period of practice would, of course, be necessary for gaining speed in signing and reading.

Two disadvantages are admitted, (1) that the system is at present unfamiliar except to the born deaf and, (2) that no system exists at present by which the manual gestures could be put into script or could be recorded, except by photography.

This suggested solution does not conform to any of the 'minimum requirements' of an auxiliary means of communication. The sign language cannot be used for written communication and it is inadequate for scientific purposes. It is, in fact, no language proper but an auxiliary means of visual communication.

A code of movements has its uses (flag signals in maritime traffic), it may even serve as a temporary expedient, an improvization among nationals of different languages. As a language, however, it is a rather primitive auxiliary which offers no prospects for serious development as a means in direct and written communication. Professor R. A. Wilson in *The Miraculous Birth of Languages* (Guild Books) gives the reasons for the early use of a sign language and its development. Darwin has made three observations which show that a sign language is inferior to a written and spoken means of communication, (1) while the hands are used to give the signs, they cannot be used for any other purpose. Sound language frees the hands; (2) Speech is a more common means of communication. It can be heard in the dark, through or across walls or when the speakers cannot see each other (modern development of telephone and wireless); sign language requires light; for it to be effective no obstacles must exist between the speakers; (3) sound radiates from the speaker in all directions, while sign language is only perceptible to a limited extent. Professor Wilson adds a further limitation of sign language. If each gesture is to represent one notion, we should require as many gestures as we possess notions. The two hands cannot form this number of gestures, neither is there a means to resolve each gesture or notion into its elements as we can in written language [roots, affixes, grammatical auxiliaries].

A Picture Language. The pictorial language, known as Isotype, was evolved by a group of people in Vienna, working together in the 'Gesellschafts- und Wirtschafts-Museum,' 1925-1934, who approached the problem of communication from an entirely new angle. The late Dr Otto Neurath, Director of the International Foundation of Visual Education, has described the principles in *International Picture Language* (Kegan Paul, 1936). The system consists of pictures representing facts and figures in a simple way, to be universally understood without further explanation. It was originally designed as a means of statistical illustration. Its elements are charts, models, lantern slides, and animated diagrams of which approximately 2,000 have been produced. Its scope is limited to the communication of facts in writing (or drawing). As Dr Neurath points out, Isotype is an auxiliary system for a group of statements which will be made clearer by pictures. It has no grammar and relies for relationship on emphasis in design. It may be used as an 'indicator', a means to communicate simple facts to the traveller in foreign parts, *e.g.*, how to use a telephone, how to read a time-table, road-signs, etc. In combination with the spoken or written word, it is an aid to understanding. It can and does reduce the complexities of statistics and text books and though it is by itself sufficient for simple statements, its value is increased by the use of ordinary speech. Isotype is a system of visual education, making no claims to equal the ordinary function of speech. As Otto Neurath says, it is not in competition with the normal languages but merely a help within its limits.

As a means in visual education its effect depends on the simplicity of its symbols. The use of colour is introduced to clarify the meaning of the statement.

The term 'auxiliary international language' (*Isotype Institute and Adult Education*, Dr Otto Neurath, Bulletin XXXI of the World Association for Adult Education) as applied to Isotype does not conform to the meaning with which it is used in this book. Ordinary language requires *definitions* for scientific purposes, firstly, because the number of terms at the disposal of the scientists are inadequate and, secondly, because the terms are not sufficiently precise.

Isotype cannot, by its very nature, fulfil the 'minimum requirements' which we demand of an international auxiliary language; it could not render any one of the three test-texts given above. I can well imagine that it would be a valuable simplification for certain purposes if used in conjunction with a planned auxiliary language. As an auxiliary means of communication it should be judged on its own merits and for the particular purpose for which it was designed.

BEGINNINGS OF A COMMON OUTLOOK

Sir Richard Gregory, Bt., F.R.S., suggested a solution to a number of problems of far-reaching importance in his address to the Seventeenth Conference of the Association of Special Libraries Information Bureaux (November 7-8, 1942). He made a survey of certain factors which have played an important part in international cooperation. In 1865 the International Telegraph Convention was held to regularize systems of transmitting telegraphic signals; in 1874 the General Postal Union was formed. The British Standards Institution, formed in 1929, regulates two kinds of standardization, (1) fundamental standards and units of measurement and, (2) industrial simplification and uniformity. Sir Richard Gregory recalled the fact that for many years new industries have tended to adopt the Metric System, a system already used in many countries of the world. At the end of the last century a conference held in Washington approved the adoption of a single prime meridian, as well as Sir Sandford Fleming's principle of dividing the whole earth into twenty-four-hour time-zones, each separated from the next by one hour. In 1875 an international conference on weights and measures fixed the standards of the international metric system which were legalized, though not enforced, in Great Britain in 1897. Today wireless wave-lengths are expressed in metres, motor car and aeroplane components in millimetres or other subdivisions of the metre, and bores of guns and similar ordnance dimensions in the same units.

There are other questions which are closely related to economic conditions which, if solved, would strengthen a common outlook.

Professor Arnold Loewenstein, the distinguished Czech eye specialist, has made a valuable suggestion which would do much to bring the peoples of Europe into closer relationship. In an interview (*Reynold's*, October 17, 1943) he mentioned that two of his country's greatest men, Jan Amos Komensky and T. G. Masaryk, worked fervently for the universality of the educational system. Komensky listed some essential conditions to attain that universality, universal books, universal schools and colleges, and a universal language. Thomas Masaryk, the first President of the free Czechoslovak Republic, continually stressed the need for an international exchange of students and an assimilation of the curricula of universities. At the time of the Renaissance, Professor Loewenstein said, Salerno, Bologna, and Prague were centres of European education. English and Russian students studied divinity, law, and medicine in Pavia. Today undergraduates begin and end their education often in the same place, thereby losing the broad outlook which they would acquire if facilities were available to continue their studies abroad.

Collaboration, in spite of political, economic, and linguistic frontiers, is the only possible alternative to further conflicts. A new outlook, far wider and broader, will be the outcome of such cooperation to which a common planned language should be the key.

The Committee on Post-War Education of the British Association has recognized the necessity of a wider education which regards the whole of Europe as an entity. The recommendations in its interim report, under section 7, are made in that spirit and propose a solution of the linguistic problem:

> *International Communication.* Apart altogether from the academic study of language and literature, every university should require its students to be able to make themselves understood, by speech and writing, in some one auxiliary means of international communication.

The Editors added the following observations which are of interest to us:

> This is not a question of learning another language but of devoting one long vacation to the acquisition of an auxiliary means of communication. Basic English, for instance, has only 850 words, whereas the English language contains 240,000, while French has 100,000, and Italian 80,000 words. A sufficient acquaintance with Basic English could be obtained in a few days by the very many post-war students who will be able to talk English. Some such means of communication is needed in the interests of 'international communication and the free interchange of ideas.' Professional diplomats can, of course, transact their business in a common language. Since it ceased to be

Latin it has generally been French and is likely, in future, to be English. English is one of the two languages of the Anglo-Soviet treaty and the common language of Generalissimo Chiang Kai-shek and the peoples of India. The last century saw a steady increase in the number of international conferences where the delegates represented not Governments or Foreign Offices, but unofficial bodies of persons interested in some aspect of science, art, law, industry, commerce, human welfare, or social justice. Such unofficial conferences are likely to be more frequent after the war. Skilled interpreters enable all the delegates to grasp what is going on in the actual conference chamber. But, when the delegates meet each other socially, they may not be able to understand each other; and yet their informal talks might do more than set speeches to promote the success of their conference as well as 'international co-operation and a free interchange of ideas.'

The desirability of promoting the introduction of an auxiliary language as an international means of communication was given particular attention after the World War of 1914-18, and the position and prospects of this subject were surveyed in a report of a British Association Committee published in 1921. In order to present the problem in a comprehensive manner, the Committee communicated with leading authorities and associations having special knowledge of classical and modern languages as well as interest in the use of an international auxiliary language. The particular claims of three types of such a language were stated, namely:

   (i) A dead language, *e.g.*, Latin.
  (ii) A national language, *e.g.*, English.
 (iii) An invented or artificial language, *e.g.*, Esperanto and Ido.

The advantages and disadvantages of each of these types were considered by the Committee, and as the result of this analysis, the following conclusions were reached:

   (i) Latin is too difficult to serve as an international auxiliary language.

  (ii) The adoption of any modern national language would confer undue advantages and excite jealousy.

 (iii) Therefore an invented language is best. Esperanto and Ido are suitable; but the Committee is not prepared to decide between them.

Since the publication of the British Association's report twenty-one years ago, the great political changes which have taken place—or which will have taken place when the United Nations have emerged victorious from the present struggle—point to the fact that any auxiliary means of communication will have to be closely related to the English language and to be such that the learning of it is a direct step towards learning English. The Universities Bureau of the British Empire, and the new Association of University Professors and Lecturers of Allied Countries in Great Britain, could very appropriately assist in promoting the movement for an auxiliary means of international communication by preparing a report on the question whether Basic English is suitable for the purpose, and, if not, what alternative is to be preferred.

The interim report on post-war education is signed by over twenty distinguished scientists. Their recommendation cannot be ignored by any serious student of the problem as it represents the collective opinion of men of science and letters. In reviewing these recommendations, *Nature* (January 23, 1943) adds these words, 'There is, therefore, much to be said in favour of the proposal made by the British Association Committee on Post-War University Education that the learning of an international auxiliary language would best be undertaken as a long vacation study in the university (and presumably in evening classes by non-university students).'

Professor Margaret Schlauch has touched upon the problem of a constructed language in her book *The Gift of Tongues* (Allen & Unwin, 1943), discussing it in connexion with the claims that a universal language will promote international peace. It is unfortunate that enthusiasts have often claimed that an artificial language would bring about the brotherhood of peoples. This is an idealistic view which has often been proved wrong. A planned language is but an instrument which may be put to good or bad use and should consequently be judged on these merits alone. The endeavour to use a planned language to promote international friendship is incidental though it may be salutary, but whatever purpose we, as individuals, have in view, the formulation of the language should be regarded as a purely linguistic task to be solved in cooperation with philologists who have, as Professor Schlauch points out, not yet considered it a part of their study. 'The imperfections of ordinary speech have already attracted attention from some few independent spirits zealous for logic and symmetry. Their creative impetus has taken the form of elaborating perfect "artificial" languages, freed of the inconsistencies and anomalies marring even the most advanced of civilized languages. In intervals between world wars, attempts have been made to disseminate the study of Esperanto, Ido, Volapük, and other artificial languages as an aid to international communication. Those persons who expected to foster international amity by purely linguistic means have been repeatedly doomed to bitter disappointment as war after war has swept away the frail filaments of correspondence in these languages extending over national boundaries. We have seen more than once the demonstration of their insufficiency— taken alone—in promoting brotherhood among peoples. But they have served practical purposes creditably, within limits. They have facilitated the functioning of international congresses and the written communications of scientists. . . . When peace comes this problem ought to be seriously discussed. Professional linguists may be little interested as scientists, since they conceive their study to be limited to a factual analysis of languages as they are; but they may be persuaded to consider the problem as citizens of the world.' As Professor Schlauch points out, few philologists have taken a serious interest so far in the problem, but the world will look to them not to remain interested in the purely analytical study of language but to contribute, out of their vast knowledge, to the construction of a truly international language.

Professor Otto Jespersen has taken an active part in the international language movement from its inception. He testifies not only to his active support but asserts that the standard type of a planned language has been found, 'all recent attempts show an unmistakable family likeness, and may be termed dialects of one and the same type of international language. This shows that just as bicycles and typewriters are now nearly all of the same type, which was not the case with the early makes, we are now in the matter of international language approaching the time when one standard type can be fixed authoritatively in such a way that the general structure will remain stable, though new words will, of course, be constantly added when need requires.' (*An International Language*, Allen & Unwin.)

THE STAGES IN INTRODUCING A PLANNED LANGUAGE

The introduction of the language will have to pass through consecutive stages, (1) the determination of the language which shall conform to standards acceptable to scientific and social requirements, (2) the official sanction of the language selected, (3) the creation of a linguistic body to supervise the further development of the language in accordance with the principles laid down. A further step relates to the methods of teaching, (a) the selection, adoption, or adaptation of a modern method of teaching, particularly suited to a logical, planned language. This may necessitate experimental courses, word counts, and the teaching of a limited number of words for elementary and advanced courses. Such a method will have to be evolved in close collaboration with the educational bodies of the countries concerned and with due regard to former educational standards. The limited vocabulary, to be taught in all countries, will equip all students with an equivalent knowledge which should prove of mutual benefit from the very beginning; (b) a special course which assumes knowledge of one or several foreign languages could be given to tutors who wish to qualify as teachers of the auxiliary language. A Language Institute or Commission will then be able to organize systematic vacational classes.

An agreement between all contracting countries to add to all scientific books and international documents a comprehensive summary of contents in a planned language would greatly enhance its immediate value.

1. Esperanto (1887) by L. Zamenhof

I—1. History

THE AUTHOR OF THE language known as *Esperanto* was an eye-specialist, Dr Lazarus Ludovic Zamenhof, born in 1859 in Bielostok (then Russian Poland). Dr Zamenhof has told of the birth of his language in a letter addressed to M Borovko, later published in *La Lingvo Internacia*, 1896, and other publications. His native village was divided into four quarters with different languages, the Russian, Polish, German, and Jewish quarters. In order to remedy the mutual hatred accentuated by language differences, he wanted to create a neutral language to facilitate understanding between these different peoples. It was to be a language based on the living national tongues.

First Zamenhof thought of reviving one of the classic languages, but soon gave this up as impracticable. During his studies in Warsaw he began to understand the difficulties of the grammar of a living language which lead him to think of the principles for its thorough simplification. He then faced the difficulties of creating a vast vocabulary. He found that, by employing a number of affixes, one could derive a great number of words from a single root. If these elements could be brought into proper relationship much effort in memorizing new words could be saved, but all elements had to be regular and invariable. He then studied the relation between words and word elements to discover invariable affixes. If he had first hoped to create a vocabulary based on invariable elements, arbitrarily putting them into regulated relationship, he soon abandoned this idea, for the modern languages already contained a number of words in common international use. He accepted them, basing his selections on the Romanic and Germanic languages.

Right from the year 1878, while still at school, he was working on a 'lingwe universala' which he practised with his comrades, soon to be forgotten by them. While at university he re-examined and improved his language in many details. Finally, having tried in vain for two years to find a publisher for his work, he decided to publish in July 1887 his first booklet under the pen-name of *Doktoro Esperanto*, which later became the name of the language itself.

His project was originally conceived as an *a priori* (*i.e.*, theoretical) language though many *a posteriori* (*i.e.*, natural) elements were taken from the living languages. He tried to attain (1) the principle of the greatest conceivable internationality of the roots and (2) the principle of the invariability of the elements contained in the vocabulary.

As soon as Zamenhof had tested his language and experimented with it for several years, he decided to submit it to the judgment of scientists. He did not want to be the creator, but only the initiator of the international auxiliary language. He knew that the work of one man could not be perfect in every detail. In 1888 he decided to change nothing in his language but to collect all criticism, to discuss and afterwards to correct, his work, until finally he could give definite shape to the language. At that time he was prepared to confide this work to an academy which would take charge of this task. In 1896 Zamenhof proposed a 'congress of written opinions' to decide the question of an international language (L. Zamenhof, *Choix d'une langue internationale*, 1896). The attempts to find a solution of the problem made little headway because the people interested were divided on the question of the choice among several systems (*Volapük, Novilatin, Veltparl*, etc.). Zamenhof suggested unity among all interested persons and bodies, and proposed an impartial enquiry to choose one system which should serve as a basis for the final language. At that time he declared himself ready to accept the decision of the majority, though the scepticism and inertia of the public had yet to be conquered.

The 'language of Dr Esperanto' found adherents, first in Russia where the society *Espero* was founded in St. Petersburg in 1892, then in Germany where Leopold Einstein, a well-known interlinguist, was the president of a club in Nuremberg, founded in 1885 in support of Volapük. The first journal, *La Esperantisto*, started in September 1889. Henry Phillips, secretary of the *American Philosophical Society* and R. Geoghegan, British Consul in Washington, started propaganda in the English-speaking world. Grammars, vocabularies, and literature were soon ready in many languages (Swedish, Polish, Lettish, Danish, Czech, Bulgarian, Italian, Spanish, Portuguese, and Hebrew).

When the Russian censorship suppressed *La Esperantisto* because it published an article by Tolstoy, it was replaced by *Lingvo Internacia* published in Upsala, Sweden. Lively propaganda started in *L'Étranger* and in *L'Indépendance Belge*; the adherence of Louis de Beaufront, himself the author of an international language system, *Adjuvanto*, greatly accelerated its diffusion. As soon as de Beaufront heard of Esperanto, a language he considered superior to his own project, he discarded Adjuvanto. In 1898 at Épernay he founded *L'Espérantiste* and the *Société pour la propagation de l'Espéranto* and soon published a number of manuals, readers, and propaganda booklets. A Canadian group of Esperantists started *L'Espérantiste Canadien*, later to be called *La Lumo*. The further diffusion of the language was secured, societies and groups sprang up in most countries.

The literature on and in Esperanto has now risen to many thousands of translated and original works, periodicals are published on all kinds of subjects including science, art, and education. The number of people using the language before 1939 has been variously estimated and certainly exceeded 100,000 practising Esperantists. Esperanto has proved, in its original form, its usefulness as a means for communication in many international congresses, held annually prior to the war 1914-18 in many different countries and has been used for commerce and travel, for science, and to some extent for business purposes. The Esperanto movement is today the greatest single group practising an auxiliary language and is bound to influence to an appreciable degree the future shape of the planned auxiliary language.

I—2. *Grammar*

The *alphabet* comprises 27 letters, five vowels and twenty-two consonants. All vowels are pronounced separately, *a* [pronounced as in *father*], *e* [*veil*], *i* [*machine*], *o* [*most*], *u* [*rule*]. *Ĵ* and *ŭ* are semi-consonants, *j* in -*oj* and -*aj* being pronounced as in *boy* and *ŭ* as in *away*. The consonants are *b, c, ĉ, d, f, g, ĝ, h, ĥ, j, ĵ, k, l, m, n, p, r, s, ŝ, t, [ŭ], v, z*. The pronunciation of the following consonants differs from English usage: *c* [always as *ts*], *g* [*gold*], *ĝ* [*gem*], *ĥ* [*loch*], *j* [*yes*], *ĵ* [*journal*], *s* [*house*], *ŝ* [*she*], *z* [*organize*]. In the two diphthongs [*aŭ, eŭ*] the letter *ŭ* is not pronounced separately [*aŭskult/i, Eŭrop/o*].

The *word-stress* or *tonic accent* falls in polysyllabic words always on the penultimate syllable, a diphthong counting as a syllable [*doktor/o, gard/i*].

The *definite article* is *la* for all genders and numbers [*la ruĝaj floroj estas grandaj*].

The *noun* in singular ends in -*o*, a -*j* is added for the plural [*la staci/o, la staci/oj* = the station].

The *personal pronouns* are *mi, vi, li, ŝi, ĝi; ni, vi, ili, oni*. The reflexive pronoun is *si*.

The *possessive pronouns* are formed by adding -*a*, [*mi-a, vi-a*, etc.].

The *verb* in the infinitive ends in -*i* [*am/i* = to love].

The *present indicative* or present tense ends in -*as* for all numbers [*mi am/as, ni am/as*].

The *past tense* ends in -*is* for all numbers [*am/is*].

The *future tense* ends in -*os* [*am/os*].

The *conditional tense* ends in -*us*. The *imperative, optative*, and *hortative* ends in -*u* [*li am/us, am/u*].

The *passive voice* is formed with the verb *est/i* = to be, followed by the passive participle [*mi estas amata* = I am loved, *mi estis amata* = I was loved].

The *conjugation* of *est/i* [to be] is:

present tense	past tense	future tense
mi estas	mi estis	mi estos
vi (ci) estas	vi (ci) estis	vi (ci) estos
li estas	li estis	li estos
ŝi estas	ŝi estis	ŝi estos
ĝi estas	ĝi estis	ĝi estos
ni estas	ni estis	ni estos
vi estas	vi estis	vi estos
ili estas	ili estis	ili estos

The *participles:*

	active participles end in	passive participles end in
present tense	*-anta* [mi estas am/anta]	*-ata* [mi estas am/ata]
past tense	*-inta* [am/inta]	*-ita* [am/ita]
future tense	*-onta* [am/onta]	*-ota* [am/ota]

The *adjectives* have the grammatical ending *-a* in singular, and *-aj* in plural [*la bona patro* = the good father, *la bonaj patroj*].

The *adverb* ends in *-e* [*bel/e kanti* = to sing beautifully].

The *cardinal numbers* are: *unu, du, tri, kvar, kvin, ses, sep, ok, naŭ, dek; cent; mil. Ducent* 200, *naŭcent* 900.

The *ordinal numbers* are formed by adding *-a, unu/a, du/a, tri/a,* etc.

The *degrees of comparison* are *pli* and *plej* [*bona, pli bona, plej bona; bela, malpli bela, malplej bela*].

Syntax: The accusative is formed by adding *-n*, and is used to express: (1) the direct object [*mi amas ŝin* = I love her, *obei la patron* = to obey the father, *kion vi bezonas* = what do you require], (2) to replace an omitted preposition, particularly with complements indicating the date, the duration, the measure, and the price [*la lastan fojon* = last time; *alta kvin futojn* = five foot high; *mi restos tri tagojn* = I will remain for three days; *tiu ĉi libro kostas ses frankojn* = this book costs six francs], (3) to indicate movement or direction to, if the preposition does not clearly express the aim [*mi iras Parizon* = I am going to Paris; *la kato saltas (sur) la tablon* = the cat jumps onto the table; *antaŭen* = forward]. In all other cases the prepositions are followed by the nominative. The prepositions *al* and *ĝis* are always followed by the nominative. The interrogative phrase begins with *ĉu*, or any other interrogative pronoun or adverb [*kial, kiu, kiam*]. Inversion does not make a phrase interrogative. The general word order is not fixed by grammatical rules. The usual order is subject-verb-object. The adjective may precede or follow the noun which it qualifies. The preposition always precedes the noun [*kun miaj tri plej bonaj amikoj* = with my three best friends.].

The table of *correlative words* contains 45 words which are *a priori* in definition and relationship. They are particles of arbitrary but regular formation, having reference to objects, persons, number, time, and place. They are formed by combining fourteen elements with five beginnings and nine endings each with a definite meaning.

	Indefinite Some (any)	Interrogative or Relative Which, what	Demonstrative That	Universal Each, every, all	Negative No
QUALITY kind sort	*ia* of some kind some (kind of)	*kia* of what kind what kind of what a..!	*tia* of that kind that kind of such a..	*ĉia* of every kind every kind of	*nenia* of no kind no kind of
MOTIVE reason	*ial* for some reason	*kial* for what reason, why, wherefore	*tial* for that reason, therefore, so	*ĉial* for every reason	*nenial* for no reason
TIME	*iam* at some time, ever	*kiam* at what time, when	*tiam* at that time, then	*ĉiam* at every time, at all times, always	*neniam* at no time, never
PLACE	*ie* in some place, somewhere	*kie* in what place, where	*tie* in that place, there, yonder	*ĉie* in every place, in all places, everywhere	*nenie* in no place, nowhere
MANNER way	*iel* in some way, somehow	*kiel* in what way, how, as	*tiel* in that way, thus, so, as, like that	*ĉiel* in every way	*neniel* in no way, nohow
POSSESSION —one's	*ies* someone's, somebody's	*kies* which one's, whose	*ties* that one's	*ĉies* everyone's, each one's, everybody's	*nenies* no one's, nobody's
THING	*io* something, aught	*kio* what thing, what	*tio* that thing, that	*ĉio* everything, all	*nenio* nothing, naught
QUANTITY amount	*iom* some quantity, somewhat	*kiom* what quantity, how much, how many	*tiom* that quantity, so { much as { many	*ĉiom* the whole quantity, all of it	*neniom* no quantity, not a bit, none
INDIVIDU-ALITY one	*iu* someone, some (person or thing)	*kiu* which (one), who	*tiu* that (one)	*ĉiu* every (one), each (one), everybody	*neniu* no (one), nobody

International words which the majority of languages have taken from a common source, undergo no change in Esperanto except that by which they conform to its orthography. With various words derived from a common root, however, it is recommended to use unchanged only the root and to form all other words from it in accordance with the rules of Esperanto (*Rule 15, Grammar of Esperanto*).

I—3. Derivation and affixes

According to rule 11 of Zamenhof's grammar, all word-elements (roots, affixes, and terminations), are independent of each other, invariable, monosignificant, in form as well as in meaning. The grammatical meaning of each element remains the same in all combinations. Esperanto uses indirect derivation (use of affixes) and direct derivation (interchangeability of grammatical terminations). We may

add to the root any grammatical termination to obtain respectively
the noun in singular [-*o*], the noun in plural [-*oj*], the infinitive [-*i*],
the adjective [-*a*], or the adverb [-*e*]. If we wish to know when to use
direct derivation (*e.g.*, the substitution of one termination for
another), or indirect derivation (*e.g.*, the insertion of the appropriate
suffix between root and termination to obtain the desired meaning),
we must know the grammatical classification of the root itself. The
root may be of verb-like, noun-like or adjective-like character. The
roots *vidv*- and *virg*- could be either verb-like = verbal, or noun-
like = substantival; we therefore have to refer to Zamenhof's dictionary which translates *vidv*- as 'widower', and *virg*- as 'virginal',
the first being a substantival root and the second an adjectival root.
Consequently we can derive *vidv/a*, *vidv/o*, by simply substituting
the termination -*o* for -*a*; in the second case we have to derive
virg/ul/in/o = virgin, *ul* indicating 'a person characterized by'. In
most cases the grammatical category of the root is obvious, in doubtful cases it is decided by reference to Zamenhof's dictionary and by
international usage.

For the purpose of indirect derivation in Esperanto, the *Lingva
Komitato* has accepted the principle of *necessity and sufficiency*, formulated by R. de Saussure in his *Construction logique des mots en
Esperanto* (1910): 'The formation of any constructed word is obtained by combining all the word elements (roots, affixes, and terminations) which are *necessary* and *sufficient* to evoke clearly the
idea to be represented.'

Starting from *martel/o* = the hammer, we can derive *martel/ad/o*
= hammering [F *martelage*] using the suffix -*ad*- to indicate the
verbal sense of action as the root *martel*- does not express the sense
of action. In substituting the infinitive ending -*i* for -*o* we obtain the
verb [*martel/ad/i*]. As all verbs express action we may now dispense
with the suffix -*ad*- added to the verb [*martel/i*]. If we insist on
using it, we express the sense of action twice and, according to de
Saussure's rule of necessity and sufficiency, this is superfluous.

Similarly the suffix -*ec*- may or may not be inserted after adjectival
roots [*bel/a* = beautiful, *bel(ec)/o* = beauty, *bel/ul/o* = beautiful
person; *ver/a* = true, *ver(ec)/o* = truth; *util/a* = useful, *util(ec)/o* =
usefulness].

A number of other affixes submit to the same rule [*pun/i* = to
punish, *pun(ad)/o* = punishment; *konstru/i* = to construct, *konstru-
(aĵ)/o* = building; *skrib/i* = to write, *skrib(aĵ)/o* = a written thing,
document].

According to Zamenhof's grammar, rule 11 (*Fundamenta Krestomatio*), affixes may be used as full and independent words with the
appropriate grammatical termination. Karl Minor has made a
thorough study of the correct use of affixes as word-building elements and as independent units in *Esperanto-Deutsches Handwörterbuch* (Ellersiek & Borel G.m.b.H., Berlin, 1924) *Endungen, Nach-
silben, Affixe*, pp. 3-71. -*ul*- denotes a person characterized by

[*bel/ul/in/o* = a beautiful woman, *ul/et/o* = a small somebody,
D *Wicht, Männchen;* *ali/ul/o* = *ulo de aliaj karakterizaj ecoj* =
someone else]. The suffix *-ebl-* expressing possibility is independently used [*ebl/a* = possible, *ebl/e* = perhaps]. The suffix *-uj-* is used to
indicate a container [*uj/o*]. The preposition *ne*, also used as a prefix
to indicate negation, may become a verb by adding the ending *-i*
[*ne/i* = to negate, analogically *jes/i* = to affirm].

PREFIXES

bo-	denotes relationship by marriage [*bo/patro* = father-in-law, *bo/frato* = brother-in-law]
dis-	denotes separation, dispersal [*dis/doni* = to distribute]
ek-	denotes commencement, suddenness, brief duration of action [*ek/krii* = to exclaim]
eks-	denotes ex-, late, formerly [*eks/reĝo* = ex-king, *eks/ministro* = former minister]
ge-	denotes both sexes taken together [*ge/patroj* = father and mother]
mal-	denotes the direct opposite [*mal/granda* = small, *mal/helpi* = to impede, to prevent]
mis-	denotes an erroneous or wrong action [*mis/uzi* = to misuse]
re-	denotes back, again [*re/sendi* = to send back, *re/pagi* = to reimburse]

Prepositions may be used as prefixes.

SUFFIXES

-aĉ-	denotes derogatory meaning [*virin/aĉ/o* = a hag]
-ad-	used to derive the verb from a substantival root [*bros/ad/i* = to brush]; if the root is verbal, shows continuation [*rid/ad/i* = keep on laughing]
-aĵ-	denotes concrete object or thing, possessing the quality of, or made out of [*ov/aĵ/o* = an omelette, *konstru/aĵ/o* = building]
-an-	denotes an inhabitant, member, partisan of [*Pariz/an/o* = a Parisian, *an/o* independently used denotes a member]
-ar-	denotes a whole formed through a collection of units [*vort/ar/o* = dictionary, *ŝtup/ar/o* = staircase]
-ebl-	denotes possibility [*tuŝ/ebl/a* = tangible]
-ec-	denotes the abstract state or quality [*bon/ec/o* = goodness; *jun/ec/o* = youth]
-eg-	denotes augmentation, intensity, a high degree [*dom/eg/o* = mansion, *varm/eg/a* = hot]
-ej-	denotes the place, of, for, etc. [*lern/ej/o* = school]
-em-	denotes inclination to [*babil/em/a* = talkative]
-er-	denotes a unit of a collective whole [*mon/er/o* = a coin; *sabl/er/o* = a grain of sand]
-estr-	denotes head of [*ŝip/estr/o* = a ship's captain]
-et-	forms diminutives [*rid/et/i* = to smile, *varm/et/a* = lukewarm]
-id-	denotes descendant, young of [*ĉeval/id/o* = a foal]
-ig-	denotes to cause something to be done [*sci/ig/i* = to make known; *la suno brunigas la homan haŭton* = the sun causes the human skin to turn brown]
-iĝ-	denotes to become and should be differentiated from *-ig-* [*mi fermis la pordon* = I closed the door, or *la pordo ferm/iĝ/is; kon/iĝ/i* = to become known]

-il-   denotes a tool or implement [*hak/il/o* = axe] and is often used as an
            independent word meaning instrument
-in-   denotes female sex [*kok/in/o* = hen]
-ind-   denotes worthy of [*laŭd/ind/a* = praiseworthy]
-ing-   denotes holder of an object, socket [*kandel/ing/o* = candlestick]
-ism-   denotes distinctive doctrine, system of thought, cult [*ideal/ism/o* =
            idealism; *social/ism/o* = socialism]
-ist-   denotes a person habitually occupied with [*art/ist/o* = artist]
-uj-   denotes a container or receptacle, often used as an independent
            word [*suker/uj/o* = sugar-basin]; also forms names of lands from
            roots denoting a race [*Angl/uj/o* = England]
-ul-   denotes a person characterized by [*bel/ul/in/o* = a beauty]
-um-   an indefinite suffix [*plen/um/i* = to fulfill; *mastr/um/i* = to manage
            a household]

The suffixes -*ĉj*- (masculine) and -*nj*- (feminine) may be added to a name,
or part of it, to express endearment.

NUMERICAL SUFFIXES

-obl-   denotes multiplied by [*du/obl/a* = *double*]
-on-   denotes fraction of [*tri/on/o* = one third]
-op-   denotes numerical collective [*kvin/op/e* = in fives, five together]
            Several affixes may be added to one root [*mal/varm/eg/a* = icecold].

I—4. *Vocabulary*

Dr Zamenhof tried to reduce his vocabulary to a small number of
roots which had been chosen mainly from German, English, French,
Polish, and Russian. The selection of a number of regular affixes
gave his language a great flexibility. His original *Universala Vortaro*
contained 2,629 roots (Stojan's count). In the six *Aldonoj* (Supplements) the Lingva Komitato introduced a number of new roots
required, and with certain words used by Zamenhof in his later
works, the total number of official Esperanto roots inclusive of the
recognised neologisms now exceeds 6,000. To that should be added
those roots which may be used according to rule 15 of his grammar,
'the so-called *foreign* or *international words*'—that is, those which
the majority of languages have taken from one source or another—
undergo no change in Esperanto, beyond conforming to its orthography; 'but with various words from one root, it is better to use
unchanged only the fundamental word and to form the rest from
this latter in accordance with the rules of the Esperanto language.'

Couturat and Leau divide the Esperanto vocabulary (*Histoire de la
Langue Universelle*, 1907) into three main groups, (1) those roots
which are already internationally known (in countries of European
civilization) and which Zamenhof adopted with phonetic spelling
conforming, as far as possible, to their etymological origin [*atom,
aksiom, bark, danc, form, flut, fosfor, panter, paraliz, poŝt, teatr, tabak,
tualet, vagon*]. This category contains a great many scientific terms,
which were, however, not contained in the *Universala Vortaro*
[*filologio, filozofio, fiziko, poezio, poeto, profesoro, doktoro, komedio,
literaturo, tragedio, telegrafo, lokomotivo*, etc.], (2) those words which

were partially international, *i.e.*, which were used in several but not in all countries of European civilization. Here Zamenhof chose the most internationally known form which was common to the greatest number of ethnic languages [*flam, marŝ, mast* (DEFIRS)[1], *ankr* (DEFIR), *benk* (DEFIS), *marmor* (DFIRS), *jun, artiŝok, fason* (DEFR), *anonc* (DEFI), *mus* (DEIR), *bind, blind, dank, fajr, fiŝ, fingr, glas, help, jar, land, melk, rajt, ring, send, ŝip, sun, trink, varm, verk, vort* (DE)], (3) those terms for which a common, international word did not exist. Here Zamenhof took the roots from the main ethnic languages or from Latin [*sed, tamen, apud, dum, aŭd, brak, dors, dekstr, feliĉ, proksim*]. He took a number of roots of purely Germanic origin [*bedaŭr, bird, fraŭl, flik, knab, kugl, ŝajn, silk, ŝirm, ŝraub, ŝut, taŭg, vip*], and a number of Slavonic origin [*bulk, brov, prav, ŝelk, svat, vost*]. All those words were adapted to conform to his phonetic and grammatical rules. Through the use of a number of invariable affixes, the use of this limited vocabulary was greatly increased. The very extensive use made of the prefix *mal-* alone increases the vocabulary by several hundred words (*Esperanto-Ido Dictionary*, London, 1934). Word formation in Esperanto is regular and the student who learns one root can put this root to many different uses [*parol-, parol/i, parol/o, parol/a, parol/e, parol/ant/o,* etc.] by using invariable grammatical terminations and affixes.

I—5. Comparative texts

(*The Emperor's New Clothes, by Hans Christian Andersen*).

'Mia Dio!' li pensis, 'ĉu eble mi estas stulta? Tion mi neniam supozis, kaj tion neniu devas ekscii. Ĉu mi ne taŭgas por mia ofico? Ne, estus netolereble, ke mi diru, ke mi ne vidas la teksaĵon!'

'Nu, vi diras nenion pri ĝi!' diris unu el la teksistoj.

'Ho, ĝi estas belega, tute ĉarma!' diris la maljuna ministro, rigardante tra siaj okulvitroj, 'tiu desegno kaj tiuj koloroj! Jes, mi diros al la imperiestro, ke ĝi tre plaĉas al mi!'

'Nu, tio plezurigas nin!' diris la du teksistoj, kaj ili nomis la kolorojn kaj la eksterordinaran desegnon.

La maljuna ministro aŭskultis atente, por ke li povu diri la saman, kiam li revenos al la imperiestro, kaj tion li faris.

(*Comparative Texts, International Auxiliary Language Association* (*IALA*).)

(*A text written by L. L. Zamenhof, Foreword to the fifth edition of the Fundamenta Krestomatio*, 1907.)

Mi trarigardis denove la tutan Krestomation kaj mi forigis el ĝi ĉiujn preserarojn kiujn mi trovis. Dum la trarigardado mi trovis diversajn esprimojn, kiuj siatempe ŝajnis al mi bonaj, sed kiuj nun al mi ne plaĉas kaj kiujn mi volonte ŝanĝus; mi tamen tion ĉi *ne* faris, ĉar mi estas konvinkita, ke por verko, kiu havas la celon subtenadi uniformecon de stilo inter ĉiuj esperantistoj, severa konstanteco

[1] D (German), E (English), F (French), I (Italian), R (Russian), S (Spanish).

estas multe pli grava ol plena perfekteco, kaj la utilo de la faritaj
ŝanĝoj estus multe pli malgranda ol la malutilo, kiun ni recevus, se
mi en ĉiu nova eldono de la Krestomatio volus fari ŝanĝojn laŭ mia
plej nova opinio aŭ gusto kaj se ĉiu posedanto de la Krestomatio
devus timi, ke nova eldono senvalorigis la malnovan.

Ĉar la Krestomatio enhavas tre grandan kvanton de materialo, kiu
estis verkita en diversaj tempoj kaj de diversaj aŭtoroj, tial ne estas
mirinde, ke en la libro troviĝas kelkaj vortoj aŭ esprimoj, kiuj ne en
ĉiuj lokoj sonas absolute egale (ekzemple: Jesuo kaj Jezu, Kanadujo
kaj Kanado, iri returnen kaj returne, k.t.p.)[2]. Ĉar ne venis ankoraŭ la
tempo, por diri la lastan vorton pri tiuj dubaj formoj, tial mi preferis
ne tuŝi tiujn duoblajn formojn, sed rigardi *ambaŭ* formojn kiel egale
bonajn kaj uzeblajn laŭ la libera elekto de la uzantoj.

I—6. Commentary

Esperanto is today the only artificial language which has been able
to form and to maintain a mass movement. The literature of the
language is wide and varied, classics have been translated into it and
scientific works of repute have appeared in Esperanto. A great
number of periodicals on various subjects besides those propagating
the language have been published throughout the world. International congresses have been held in most of the European capitals
establishing the practical value of the spoken system. Through the
persistent propaganda work of its supporters, the name *Esperanto* has
in many minds become a synonym for *international auxiliary
language*.

Esperanto has often been subjected to criticism. In spite of it, it
has proved its usefulness. Improvements could, however, be made,
particularly if we compare recent interlinguistic studies and the
experiences gained from other systems, partially or wholly based on
Esperanto.

We should have to write the full history of Dr Zamenhof's language in order to understand the reasons why its author has withheld
certain changes in his language which he himself carefully collected,
examined, and published in 1894 in *Esperantisto*. A system which
had to fight its way against the indifference of the public had, in Dr
Zamenhof's opinion, to maintain an internal stability. At the first
Esperanto-Congress at Boulogne-sur-Mer, France, in August 1905,
the Esperantists decided that the basis of the language as contained
in the 'Fundamento' should remain valid, until the language was
officially recognized and adopted. Esperanto has consequently never
been, and is not today, open to fundamental changes or adjustments
based on new proposals in the field of interlinguistics, though it does
develop according to its own laws.

Zamenhof's most striking innovation was the accent ^ which is
not used in the same way in any other language. It is a reversal of
the Czech accent ˅ and was used for five different letters. These

---

[2] Usage has now decided for *Jesuo, Kanado, returne.*

supersigns were introduced to make Esperanto fully phonetic though they were a stumbling block in the first years of propaganda for Esperanto when printers did not possess these signs. Anticipating this difficulty, Zamenhof admitted that an 'h' may be put after the letter which should normally carry the accent if this accent is unobtainable [ĝ = gh]. The letter ĥ (guttural *ch* as in *loch*) violates the principle that the planned language should not contain any sounds which offer difficulties to European peoples [*monarĥo, ĥronologio, ĥirurgio, ĥemio*]. In Ido it has been replaced by the sound *k* [*monarko, kronologio, kirurgio, kemio*]. The letters ĉ and ŝ were introduced to make an acceptable compromise between phonetic and historic spelling of many words common to several European languages. Some systems of I.L. have preferred to retain the historic spelling while others have sacrificed orthography to phonetic symbols. The letter ĝ serves as a good example of a successful compromise in Esperanto [*ĝardeno* = F *jardin*, D *Garten*, E *garden*, I *giardino*]. If ĝ had not been added to the Esperanto alphabet, Zamenhof would have had to write *gardeno* understood by English and Germans only, or possibly *jardino* [or *djardino*] used in the Romanic languages. *ĝardeno* is recognised by the Anglo-Saxon nations visually, *i.e.*, owing to its historic spelling, and by the Romanic nations orally, *i.e.*, owing to its sound. Although Zamenhof introduced these new letters to his alphabet he left out a letter which is internationally known as a character and a sound, *x*. In Esperanto *x* is represented either as *ks* [*ekskluzive*] or as *kz* [*ekzerco, ekzemplo*] which is unjustifiable from the historic, and doubtful from the phonetic point of view.

A very ingenious part of the grammar is the table of correlative words, but ingenious as it is, it lacks the natural elements which are familiar to many Europeans. It is largely arbitrary and artificial. In 1894 Zamenhof published a table showing words taken from the European languages or from Latin. It is interesting to see that some of the published forms were subsequently introduced into Ido.

English	Esperanto	proposed new forms	forms in Ido [3]
of every kind	ĉia	omne	omnaspeca
always	ĉiam	semper	sempre
all	ĉio	omno	omno
everybody	ĉiu	omnu	omnu
all (people)	ĉiuj	omnui	omni
when	kiam	kvandu	kande
where	kie	ubu	ube
how	kiel	kom	quale
what	kio	kvo	quo
how many (much)	kiom	kvantu	quante
of no kind	nenia	nule	nulspeca
there	tie	ibu	ibe
here	ĉi tie	hik	hike
so much	tiom	tantu	tante

[3] see Chapter II for other comparisons with Ido.

The adjective in Esperanto is variable but this variability does not add to the clarity of the language and offers no considerable advantages. Ido uses the invariable adjective [Esperanto = *la belaj floroj*, Ido = *la bela flori*]. The plural ending in *-j* which to many appears inelegant and heavy was proposed to be abolished in favour of *-i*. '*Multaj kompetentaj personoj estas konvinkitaj, ke kelkaj ŝanĝoj kaj plibonigoj estas dezirindaj kaj eĉ necesaj. Ekzemple la multaj groteskaj kaj absurdaj finaj "j" devas esti aboliciitaj.*' ('Many competent persons are convinced that some changes and improvements are desirable and even necessary. For example the many grotesque and absurd final *j*'s should be abolished.')

Many hours are spent by every student of Esperanto in learning to use the accusative form correctly. Its use is obligatory although it does in no way contribute to the clarity of the phrase except in inversion [*la Krestomatio enhavas tre grandan kvanton de materialo*]. Ido has retained the accusative but applies it only in inversion [*la patro punisas la filio* = the father punishes the son; *la filion la patro punisas* = it is the son whom the father punishes.]

THE VOCABULARY: The chief method of introducing new words into Esperanto is the unlimited admission of official or unofficial neologisms. Official, if these words have been sanctioned by the Lingva Komitato, unofficial, if they are new words coined to express some new idea or term which has arisen through scientific development in the ethnic languages and which may be used according to paragraph 15 of Zamenhof's grammar. The proper application of these neologisms may differ according to the people, national or scientific, who introduce new terms. Under *Esperantologiaj principoj* (*Esperanto-Ido*, London, 1935) I have given a few examples of such new Esperanto words which were differently translated in the English and German Esperanto-dictionaries. There may be comparatively few of such neologisms which acquire different meanings. The official vocabulary of Esperanto contains, as has already been stated, some 4,500 roots in Zamenhof's *Universala Vortaro* and six official supplements (*Aldonoj*) and 2,000 new roots used as neologisms. The Ido vocabulary contains approximately 10,000 roots exclusive of those thousands of roots which would be required to complete the necessary scientific terminologies in Ido or any other planned system. Jespersen has repeatedly emphasized the necessity of word economy saying that a planned language cannot hope to express all the subtleties of all the ethnic languages. At the same time we should not prefer economy to precision of meaning. As the Esperanto vocabulary is too restricted to cover some essential terms, it had to extend the meaning of its roots which, in Ido, are expressed by different roots. Esperanto uses the term *nom/i* for the two meanings to call, and to nominate [Ido *nom/iz/ar*, *nomin/ar*], the extended term *mal/dik/a* where Ido has *tenu/a* = tenuous, thin, fine, *magr/a* = lean, meager, lank, spare, *din/a* = thin. *Frukto-don/a* is used to cover Ido *fertil/a* = fertile, and Ido *frukto-don/ant/a* = fruit-giving, though a fertile piece of land may be uncultivated for many years. If the principles of the Esperanto vocabulary were considered the best ones, any short-comings in its present vocabulary could however easily be corrected. The selection of roots and word-building elements in Esperanto is, in many cases, unfortunate, because they form words which have a similarity with words of other ethnic languages though they are in no way related to them. The compound *foresto* [*for-est/o*] does not mean forest but means the state of being absent or away, *fraŭlo* does not mean D *Frau* or *Fräulein* but bachelor.

The purpose of this book is to give a short review of the character-istics of the chief auxiliary language systems which are of proved usefulness and the student who is interested to know more of the grammatical details of the problems should refer to the books recom-mended in the bibliography.

We have already seen that a further increase in the available word-material in Esperanto is achieved by using as independent roots the affixes of the language. The use of the suffix *-ec-* as a full word [*ec/o*] to denote the state or condition of something introduces an artificial aspect into the language. This criticism applies equally to other suffices when used independently. Although some persons contest the advisability of using affixes in this way, every Esperanto teacher would argue that their use is legitimate.

The prefix *mal-* is extensively used in Esperanto to indicate the direct opposite and it helps to reduce considerably the number of required roots. If we know that *facil/a* means easy, we also know that *mal-facil/a* means difficult, analogically *fort/a* = strong, and *mal-fort/a*, *nov/a*=new, *mal-nov/a*, *antaŭ*=before, *mal-antaŭ*. Although this is a very convenient way of expressing the direct opposite, it is overdone in Esperanto. In many cases the meaning is stretched and no longer clear [*mal-dung/i provizore* = to suspend, or *mal-dung/i* = to dismiss, from *dung/i* = to hire (a servant); *mal-ferm/i* = to open; *mal-grand/a* = small; but it admits the root *mikr-* in *mikroskop/o*; *mal-kler/ul/o* = an illiterate person, from *kler/a* = enlightened, cultured; *mal-okult/a* = exoteric; *mal-pli-mult/o* = minority; *mal-pur-ig/i* = to contaminate; *mal-venk/i* = to lose; *mal-san/o* = illness] As *mal-* has the sense of 'evil' in Latin, it is an unfortunate choice as long as the Latin meaning persists in compounds of ethnic languages.

A more detailed study of the derivation of Esperanto will be found in Chapter VIII. Although Esperanto cannot be considered the solution of the problem of communication, it will have much to con-tribute to the final form of the planned language.

II. Ido (1900-1907), *Linguo Internaciona di la Delegitaro, by Louis de Beaufront assisted by Louis Couturat and finally formulated by the Délégation pour l'adoption d'une langue internationale*

II—1. *History*

AT THE TIME OF the World Exhibition in 1900, many international scientific organizations chose Paris for their conferences and congresses. At these important meetings, attended by people from many countries, the language differences were an obvious disadvantage and were acutely felt. An eminent scientist, Léopold Leau, professor of mathematics, proposed a solution by means of an auxiliary language constructed on scientific principles. Many of those who were experiencing the difficulties of communication gave him encouragement and support. After careful preparation the *Délégation pour l'adoption d'une Langue Auxiliaire Internationale* was formed on 17th January 1901 on the initiative of Léopold Leau. The programme of this Delegation contained two important points:

(1) 'It is desirable that an international auxiliary language should be introduced which, though not intended to replace the natural languages in the internal life of nations, should be adapted to written and oral communication between persons of different mother-tongues.'

(2) 'In order to fulfil its object, such an international auxiliary language must satisfy the following conditions, (*a*) it must be capable of serving the needs of science as well as those of daily life, commerce, and general communication, (*b*) it must be capable of being easily learnt by all persons of average elementary education, especially those belonging to the civilized nations of Europe, (*c*) it must not be one of the living languages.'

Up to 1906 the Delegation had received the support of over 1,200 members of Academies and Faculties of Universities and the adherence of over 300 societies. In May 1907 the Delegation submitted the subject to the International Association of Academies in Vienna which, by twelve votes to eight with one abstention, declared itself unable to decide the problem of an international auxiliary language. In consequence the Delegation proceeded to form a working committee, and by 242 votes out of the total of 253, the following members were elected: Messrs Manuel Barrios, Dean of the Medical School of Lima, Peru, President of the Peruvian Senate; Baudouin de Courtenay, Professor of Linguistics at the University of St. Petersburg; E. Boirac, Rector of the University of Dijon, France; Ch. Bouchard, Member of the Academy of Sciences, Professor at the Paris Medical School; R. Eotvos, member of the Hungarian Academy of Sciences; W. Forster, chairman of the International Committee on Weights and Measures; Col. George Harvey, Editor of the *North American Review*; Otto Jespersen, Professor of Philology, University of Copenhagen, member of the Danish Academy of Sciences; S. Lambros, former Rector of the University of Athens; C. Le Paige, Director of the Scientific Section of the Royal Academy of Belgium, Administrator-Inspector of the University of Liège; W. Ostwald, member of the Royal Society of Sciences of Saxony, Professor Emeritus in the University of Leipzig; Hugo Schuchardt, member of the Imperial Academy of Sciences of Vienna, Professor at the University of Graz.

The Committee was completed by the co-option of Messrs Gustav Rados, of the Hungarian Academy of Sciences; W. T. Stead, editor of the London *Review of Reviews*; G. Peano, Professor of the University of Turin, member of the Academy of Sciences of Turin. As Messrs Bouchard, Harvey and Stead were unable to attend, they were represented by Messrs Rodet, Hugon and Dimnet; M Boirac was represented at some sittings by the prominent peace advocate, G. Moch; the joint secretaries of the Delegation, Messrs Couturat and Leau, became members of the Committee.

Couturat and Leau had published, in 1903, their remarkable book *Histoire de la Langue Universelle* (Hachette, 576 pp.) which reviewed more than fifty different systems of constructed languages. This book was sent to all members of the Committee before the sessions of the Delegation. It contains a detailed exposition of seventeen *a priori* systems, of twelve mixed systems, and of twenty-six *a posteriori* systems. It gives details of each system, alphabet, phonetics, grammar, sources of roots, and a critical commentary.

In October 1907 the committee met at the Collège de France at which, finally, the following decision was reached, 'None of the proposed languages can be adopted *in toto* and without modifications. The committee has decided to adopt in principle Esperanto, on account of its relative perfection, and of the many and varied applications which have been made of it, provided that certain modifications be executed by the Permanent Commission, on the lines indicated by the *Conclusions of the Report* (*Conclusions du Rapport*) of the secretaries and by the project of *Ido*, if possible in agreement with the Esperantist Linguistic Committee.' The Permanent Commission consisted now of Ostwald, Couturat, Leau, de Beaufront,

Jespersen, and Baudouin de Courtenay. A basis for the work of that commission was the *Histoire de la Langue Universelle* (1903) and its supplement *Les Nouvelles Langues Internationales* (1907) by Couturat and Leau, a detailed review of all projects known to the authors. In 1907 Couturat distributed his study *Étude sur la dérivation en Esperanto* which stated for the first time the principle of mono-significance of affixes and the principle of reversibility, *i.e.*, the possibility to deduce the meaning of the derivative from the meaning of the root and the fixed meaning of the affix or affixes, and inversely to analyse a full word consisting of root and one or more affixes and logically arrive at the meaning of the root.

During its sessions the authors of many systems appeared before the permanent commission to defend the principles of their languages but it soon became clear that an *a posteriori* project (*i.e.*, one which is based on ethnic languages) would have to be chosen, of which the most favoured systems were Esperanto, Neutral, Novlatin, and Universal. An anonymous project under the name of *Ido* was submitted which incorporated many of the reforms proposed as early as 1894, as well as the principles of derivation proposed by Couturat in his *Étude*; on the whole it was a reformed Esperanto. Many of the proposals were finally adopted by the Delegation in its language, but Jespersen points out that this project was not approved in all details, neither concerning grammar nor in the choice of words, and it differed in many points from what is now known under the name of *Ido*.

Louis de Beaufront had been chosen by Dr Zamenhof to represent Esperanto before the Permanent Commission, and a personal controversy followed when it became known that he was the author of the anonymous project. It has also been alleged that Couturat was the real author of that system. If so, and being a member of the delegation, he was prevented by its statute from submitting his own system. Undoubtedly *Ido* contained some of his ideas and avoided many mistakes which Couturat and Leau had pointed out in their *Histoire*. Whatever the personal aspect may have been, it is true to say that *Ido* as it is known today started as a reformed Esperanto, abolishing the accented letters and the plural form in -j. In *Ido* the adjectives were made invariable, the accusative was retained only in inversion, the *a priori* list of correlative words disappeared and the roots were chosen from the ethnic languages; the spelling of many roots was brought into conformity with international usage. All roots were re-examined on a scientific basis and many new ones adopted, the derivation was adapted to Couturat's proposal. The total result was that the language became more immediately comprehensible and more natural in aspect. After the adoption of reformed Esperanto, now known as Ido, a *Union of Friends of the International Language* was formed which elected an Academy (later known as the Ido Academy). In 1908 a monthly journal *Progreso* (edited by Couturat) was started which contained the linguistic discussions and the decisions of that academy. The grammars, dictionaries and text books which were revised in accordance with the decisions of the academy became available only after the 1914-18 war. These dictionaries were then and are today the most complete works of their kind for any system of planned language.

II—2. *Grammar*

The *alphabet* comprises 26 letters, five vowels and twenty-one consonants. The vowels are *a* [pr. as in *father*], *e* [*veil*], *i* [*machine*], *o* [*most*], *u* [*rule*]. The consonants are *b, c, d, f, g, h, j, k, l, m, n, p, q(u), r, s, t, v, w, x, y, z*. All vowels have a uniform pronunciation. The following differ from English usage: *c* [pr. as *ts* in *Tsar*], *g* always hard [as in *gold*], *h* is always sounded, *j* [as in *journal*], *s* is always sharp [as in *house*] while *z* is always soft [as in *housing*], *y* is a consonant only [pronounced as in *yes*]. Ido employs two digraphs, *ch* [pr. as in *church*], *sh* [as in *shall*]. The letter *q* is always used in combination with *u* and pronounced as in *queen*. Two diphthongs are used, *au* [*autoro*], and *eu* [*Europa*], the letters of both diphthongs are pronounced separately [*ah-oo, eh-oo*].

The *stress* is on the last syllable of the infinitive [*kantár*], and in all other cases on the penultimate syllable, with the exception of those words which contain either *i* or *u* before a vowel [*strádo, lámpo, tekníko,* but *famílio*].

The *definite article* is *la* for all genders and numbers. The form *le* is used to express the plural in connexion with an invariable adjective [*la reda flori esas granda* = the red flowers are large, *le blua esas mikra* = the blue ones are small]. The indefinite article is left unexpressed [*libro* = a book].

The *noun* in singular ends in -*o*, for the plural -*i* is substituted for -*o* [*la stacion-o, la stacion-i*].

The *personal pronouns* are *me, tu (vu), ilu, elu, olu; ni, vi, ili, eli, oli*. For the third person the pronouns may be contracted to *lu* and *li* to express the neuter. The reflexive pronoun is *su*.

The *possessive pronouns* are formed by adding -*a* [*me-a, tu-a (vu-a), ilu-a, elu-a, olu-a; ni-a, vi-a, ili-a, eli-a, oli-a*].

The *verb* in the infinitive ends in -*ar* [*am/ar* = to love]. The past may be expressed by -*ir*, the future may be expressed by -*or*. The past or future infinitive is rarely used.

The *present indicative* or tense ends in -*as* for all numbers [*me am/as, ni am/as*].

The *past tense* ends in -*is* for all numbers [*am/is*].

The *future tense* ends in -*os* [*am/os*].

The *conditional tense* ends in -*us*. The *imperative, optative,* and *hortative* tenses end in -*ez* [*ilu am/us; am/ez*].

The *passive voice* is formed with the verb *es/ar* = to be, followed by a passive participle [*me esas vokata* = I am called, *me esas vidata* = I am seen, *me esis vidata* = I was seen]. These forms can be contracted by using the root of *es/ar* as a suffix [*me vok/es/as, me vid/es/as, me vid/es/is*].

The *conjugation* of *es/ar*=to be, is:

	present tense	past tense	future tense
me, tu (vu), ilu, elu, olu ni, vi, ili, eli, oli }	esas	esis	esos

The *participles:*

	active participles end in	passive participles end in
present tense	-anta [me esas vok/anta]	-ata [me esas vok/ata]
past tense	-inta [vok/inta]	-ita [vok/ita]
future tense	-onta [vok/onta]	-ota [vok/ota]

The *adjectives* are invariable in number and gender [*mikra, bona*]. The grammatical ending in *-a* is optional [*bon, bel*].

Adverbs end in *-e* [*bele kantar* = to sing beautifully, *bone laborar* = to work well].

The *cardinal numbers* are: *un, du, tri, quar, kin, sis, sep, ok, non, dek, dek-e-un, dek-e-du; du-a-dek* = 20, *tri-a-dek* = 30, *cent, du-a-cent* = 200, *sis-a-cent* = 600.

The *ordinal numbers* are formed by means of the suffix *-esma* [*un/esma, du/esma, tri-a-cent e quar/esma* = 304th].

The *degrees of comparison* are *plu, maxim; min, minim* [*bona, plu bona, maxim bona; bela, min bela, minim bela*].

Syntax: The ordinary word order is subject-verb-object [*la monumento stacas avan la palaco*]. Short adjectives generally precede the noun [*bona ideo*]; long adjectives may follow the noun [*la linguo internaciona*]. Interrogative sentences begin with *kad*, or *ka* if the following word begins with a consonant [*ka vu promenos?*], or any other interrogative pronoun or adverb [*qui, qua, quo, kande, ube*]. Inversion is not used to express interrogative sentences. Negation is indicated by the word *ne* [*il ne agis lo*].

II—3. Derivation and affixes

The term *derivation* indicates the relation of words in various groups, *e.g.*, verbs, nouns, adjectives, adverbs. It is not used to indicate the etymological origin of a word.

Two principles are of special importance to the derivation of Ido, (1) the principle of monosignificance of all the word-building elements, also described as uniqueness of meaning and invariability, and (2) the principle of reversibility. The principle of *monosignificance:* Each root in Ido expresses one basic signification, modified as it may be by using different affixes [*-et/o, -il/o*] or grammatical terminations [*-ar, -o, -i, -a, -e*], each of which carries one invariable sense. One root, one meaning; one affix, one meaning. Knowing the form and meaning of a root, we can logically and clearly express all related ideas by use of the proper affix. If *labor/ar* means to work, *labor/o* is the verbal noun and indicates the act of working, *labor/ist/o* = the person professionally occupied with work, the worker, *labor/em/a* = to be inclined to work.

The principle of *reversibility:* The rule of reversibility was formulated by Couturat (*Étude sur la Derivation*): 'Every derivative must be *reversible;* that is to say, if one passes from one word to another of the same family in virtue of a certain rule, one must be able to pass inversely from the second to the first in virtue of a rule which is exactly the inverse of the preceding.' This follows logically on the principle of monosignificance.

Let us take the root *labor-* to see the application of both principles. The verbal root *labor/* expresses the action, *labor/ist/o* = worker, *labor/ist/ar/o* = a group of workers, or working class, *labor/em/a* = inclined to, willing to work, *labor/ist/al/a* = relating to workers, *anti-labor/ist/al/a legi* = laws directed against the working class; we now have a root preceded by an affix, followed by two suffixes, and one grammatical termination to indicate the adjective. The root *labor/* has retained its basic meaning, extended or restricted according to the various affixes used, it remains *monosignificant*. The process of adding affixes can now be reversed and we do, logically, return to the verbal root *labor/* from which we departed.

As a basis for each word we have the invariable stem, ordinarily termed 'root'. These roots are classed into three main groups, (1) verbal roots denoting an action [*labor/ar* = to work, *vid/ar* = to see] (2) nominal roots denoting an object [*hom/o* = man, *urbo*=town, *stul/o* = chair], (3) adjectival roots expressing a quality [*bon/a*= good, *facil/a* = easy, *bel/a* = beautiful]. Three rules should be noted which relate to the substitution of various grammatical endings, one for another:

RULE 1. The noun directly derived from the verb indicates the *state* or *action* expressed by the root [*fabrik/ar* = to manufacture, *fabrik/o* = the action of manufacturing].

RULE 2. An adjective directly derived from a noun indicates how the person, being or thing, is [*orfan/o* = orphan, *orfan/a infanto* = orphan child, *arjent/o* = silver, *arjent/a brosho* = silver brooch]. Inversely the noun may be derived from an adjective indicating the person, being or thing that is . . . [*rich/a* = rich, *rich/o* = a rich person; *blind/a* = blind, *blind/o* = a blind person; *dezert/a* = desert(ed), *dezert/o* = a desert, wilderness].

RULE 3. An adverb directly derived from an adjective indicates the manner of . . . [*bel/a* = beautiful, *bel/e* = beautifully, *agreabl/a* = agreeable], while the adverb directly derived from a noun forms a complement, expressing circumstances of time, place, quantity or means [*telefon/e parolar* = to talk by telephone].

The derivation is called indirect when we employ one or several affixes. These affixes are always followed by the appropriate grammatical termination [*labor/ist/o* = worker]. Ido employs 19 prefixes and 46 suffixes besides four numeral suffixes, all cited in the following list. Certain prepositions [*en, ek, for, kun, inter, de,* etc.] may be used as prefixes.

PREFIXES

anti-   denotes against, opposed to [*anti/bakterio* = bactericide, *anti/fashista*]

arki-   denotes arch, of eminent degree [*arki/episkopo*]

bo-   denotes relationship by marriage [*bo/fratino* = sister-in-law]

bi-   denotes two, used for scientific terms [*bi/loba* = bilobate; a number of other prefixes derived from scientific terms are used likewise, *mono-, quadri-, quinqua-, sexa-, septua-, nona*]

des-   denotes the direct opposite of the idea to which it is prefixed [*des/agreabla* = disagreeable]

dis-   denotes separation or dispersion [*dis/donar* = to distribute]

ex-   denotes ex-, late, former [*ex/rejo* = ex-king]

gala-   denotes gala-, this is properly an adjective but is used in a few instances as a prefix [*gala/festo* = gala festival]

ge-   denotes both sexes taken together [*ge/frati* = brothers and sisters]

mi-   denotes half, partly, semi-, demi- [*mi/cirklo* = half-circle, *mi/ombro* = half-shade]

mis-   denotes erroneous, wrong action [*mis/komprenar* = to misunderstand, *mis/prizentar* = to misrepresent]

ne-   denotes not, non-, un-, in-, ir- [*ne/posibla* = impossible, *ne/populara* = unpopular]

par-   denotes perfection of action [*par/lernar* = to learn thoroughly]

para-   denotes protection against, something to ward off [*para/fulmino* = lightning conductor, *para/pluvo* = umbrella]

pre-   denotes pre-, before [*pre/dicar* = to predict, *pre/datizer* = to ante-date]

pseudo- denotes pseudo, false [*pseudo/cienco* = pseudo-science]

retro- denotes retro-, backward, inverse action [*retro/tirar* = to draw back, *retro/spektar* = to look back]

ri-   denotes re-, back to an original state or position, again in the sense of repetition or restoration [*ri/elektar* = to re-elect, *ri-enirar* = to re-enter]

sen-   denotes -less, without, free from [*sen/arma* = without arms, weaponless]

SUFFIXES

-ach-   denotes derogatory meaning [*medik/acho* = quack]

-ad-   added to verbal roots denotes repetition or continuation of the act [*paf/o* = shot, *paf/ad/o* = shooting; *pens/ar* = to think, *pens/o* = thought, *pens/ad/o* = thinking]; this affix has been criticized and will be more fully examined in the chapter on derivation

-ag-   is the root of the verb *ag/ar* = to act, it denotes to act with instruments, to avoid direct derivation [*martel/o* = hammer, *martel/ag/ar* = to hammer]

-aj-   denotes an object possessing the quality of, or made out of [*ligna/j/o* = wooden thing, *lan/aj/o* = woollen thing]

-al-   denotes relating to, pertaining to, or appropriate to [*nacion/al/a* = national, *sexu/al/a* = sexual]

-*an*-   denotes a member, inhabitant or partisan of [*vilaj*/*an*/*o* = villager, *eklizi*/*an*/*o* = a member of a church, *partis*/*an*/*o* = partisan]

-*ar*-   denotes a collection, set, group of objects or beings [*hom*/*ar*/*o* = humanity, *delegit*/*ar*/*o* = delegation]

-*ari*-   denotes the object of an action, the recipient of an action, or one on whom a legal right is conferred [*pag*/*ari*/*o* = payee, *grant*/*ari*/*o* = grantee]

-*atr*-   denotes the nature of or having nearly the same appearance, qualities or characteristics [*metal*/*atr*/*a* = metallic, *sponj*/*atr*/*a* = spongy]

-*e*-   denotes of the colour of [*or*/*e*/*a* = golden, *tigr*/*e*/*a* = tiger coloured, mottled]

-*ebl*-   denotes possibility [*kred*/*ebl*/*a* = credible, *rupt*/*ebl*/*a* = breakable, *vid*/*ebl*/*a* = visible]

-*ed*-   denotes quantity which fills something, or the quantity determined by the nature of the action [*manu*/*ed*/*o* = handful, *glas*/*ed*/*o* = glassful, *glut*/*ed*/*o* = a swallow]

-*eg*-   denotes augmentation, intensity, a higher degree [*varm*/*eg*/*a* = hot, *grand*/*eg*/*a* = immense, *pluv*/*eg*/*o* = downpour]

-*em*-   denotes inclination to [*labor*/*em*/*a* = industrious, *babil*/*em*/*a* = talkative, *atak*/*em*/*a* = aggressive]

-*end*-   denotes which must be done [*pag*/*end*/*a* = which must be paid, *lekt*/*end*/*a* = which must be read]

-*er*-   denotes a person occupied in a customary though not professional activity [*fum*/*er*/*o* = smoker, *fotograf*/*er*/*o* = amateur photographer]

-*eri*-   denotes an industrial establishment [*imprim*/*eri*/*o* = printing office, *lakt*/*eri*/*o* = dairy]

-*es*-   is the root of *es*/*ar* = to be; denotes, with non-verbal roots, the state or quality, with verbal roots it denotes passive state [*malad*/*es*/*o* = illness, *qual*/*es*/*o* = quality, *exhaust*/*es*/*o* = exhaustion]

-*esk*-   denotes to begin to, become, start [*dorm*/*esk*/*ar* = to fall asleep, *labor*/*esk*/*ar* = to begin to work]

-*estr*- denotes head of [*urb*/*estr*/*o* = mayor]

-*et*-   denotes diminutives [*mont*/*et*/*o* = hill, *bel*/*et*/*a* = pretty, *varm*/*et*/*a* = tepid, lukewarm]

-*ey*-   denotes the place [*manj*/*ey*/*o* = a place to eat in, *koqu*/*ey*/*o* = kitchen]; note the difference between -*eri*- and -*ey*- [*lav*/*ey*/*o* = a place for washing, *lav*/*eri*/*o* = a washing establishment, laundry]

-*i*-   denotes the domain, province, or country [*duk*/*i*/*o* = duchy, *parok*/*i*/*o* = parish]

-*id*-   denotes descendant [*Napoleon*/*id*/*o* = descendant of Napoleon]

-*ier*-   denotes the holder [*rent*/*ier*/*o* = fundholder, *pom*/*ier*/*o* = apple-tree, *kandel*/*ier*/*o* = candlestick]

-*if*-   denotes to generate, produce, secrete [*sudor*/*if*/*ar* = to perspire, *elektr*/*if*/*ar* = to generate electricity]

-*ig*-   denotes to make, render, transform into [*petr*/*ig*/*ar* = to petrify, *bel*/*ig*/*ar* = to beautify, *rekt*/*ig*/*ar* = to straighten]; *ig*/*ar* is also used as an autonomous verb with the meaning to make, cause

-*ik*-   denotes ill of, sick with [*tuberklos*/*ik*/*a* = consumptive]

-*il*-   denotes the instrument [*paf*/*il*/*o* = shooting instrument, *telegraf*/*il*/*o* = a telegraphic instrument]

-*in*-   denotes female sex [*frat*/*in*/*o* = sister, *bov*/*in*/*o* = cow]

-ind-	with verbal roots denotes deserving to be, worthy of [*laud/ind/a* = praiseworthy, *libro lekt/ind/a* = a book worth reading]
-ism-	denotes a system, doctrine, cult [*social/ism/o* = socialism, *imperial/ism/o* = imperialism]
-ist-	denotes a person in some occupation, profession, and adherents of a party, system, or doctrine [*dent/ist/o* = dentist, *social/ist/o* = socialist]
-iv-	denotes capable of [*instrukt/iv/a* = instructive, *sugest/iv/a* = suggestive, *nutr/iv/a* = nutritive]
-iz-	denotes to cover with, supply with, furnish with, provide with [*arm/iz/ar* = to arm, *kron/iz/ar* = to crown, *sal/iz/ar* = to salt]
-oz-	denotes full of, containing, ornamented with [*por/oz/a* = porous, *kuraj/oz/a* = courageous, *joy/oz/a* = joyous]
-ul-	denotes male sex [*frat/ul/o* = = brother, *kaval/ul/o* = stallion]
-um-	this suffix is used with a few roots to form derivative meanings which other suffixes cannot logically express. It is only to be used for derivatives authorized by the academy [*kruc/um/ar* = to cross, *formik/um/ar* = to swarm]
-un-	denotes one unit of a substance which naturally consists of many such units [*sabl/un/o* = a grain of sand]
-ur-	denotes the result or product of an action [*pikt/ur/o* = picture, *imprim/ur/o* = printed matter]
-uy-	denotes a receptacle [*ink/uy/o* = inkwell, *monet/uy/o* = purse]
-yun-	from the independent root *yun/a* = young [*bov/yun/o* = calf, *han/yun/o* = pullet]

NUMERICAL SUFFIXES

-esm-	ordinal numbers [*un/esm/a*, *du/esm/a*, *tri/esm/a*]
-im-	fractions [*tri/im/a* = a third part]
-op-	distributives [*quar/op/e* = in fours, four at a time]
-opl-	multiplying suffix [*du/opl/e* = double, *tri/opl/e* = thrice], compare *-foye*, meaning time in counting [*tri/foy/e* = three times].

Note that several suffixes may be combined around one root.

II—4. *Vocabulary*

As its linguistic history shows, Ido is not a completely new system evolved from the existing languages. Its basis is Esperanto and several thousand roots have been accepted with slight or no modification from Zamenhof's vocabulary and from Idiom Neutral, a system described in *On the Choice of a Common Language* (Pitman). At the time of the publication of Ido, Esperanto had only developed a limited number of roots and it fell to the permanent commission and later to the Ido academy to introduce thousands of new roots. The Ido vocabulary contains to-day about 10,000 roots, *i.e.*, more than any other planned language system.

The roots selected were taken from the great European languages. Latin was used only to provide a root where the roots of the ethnic languages were unsuitable. The principle of monosignificance—one meaning for each root—or uniqueness of meaning as Professor Donnan terms it in his translation of *International Language and Science*, was adhered to as far as practicable. I deliberately say 'as far as practicable' because experience proves the impossibility of rigidly maintaining this principle. Critics have shown that certain terms do represent varying meanings, for example *pens/ar* means to think, *pens/o* = the act of thinking although in practice it is often used for 'the thought'. To be correct, *thought* should be given as *pensuro* but this is not done in practice. Let us examine two simple terms met with in most languages, 'house' and 'building'. An Englishman describes his dwelling as a house, while a building is something bigger than the home of a family. A German would describe a block of flats as 'Haus' and apply 'Gebäude' for a factory building. There are similar examples of such variation but as long as they do not interfere with the clear communication of thought, they will have to be admitted in the planned language. If we attempted to express every shade of meaning through a new root, we should have to use too vast and clumsy a vocabulary. Ortel, in his *Lectures on the study of language* (New York), quotes R. C. Temple as saying, 'I was forced to begin (the treatment of the agglutinative languages) where the other grammars ended, namely, with the sentence, defining *sentence* as the expression of complete meaning in language and making that the unit of language.' L. Susan Stebbing in *Thinking to Some Purpose* (Pelican) emphasizes the same contention. 'Ambiguity arises from difference of usage; there is ambiguity only so far as the difference of usage is not noticed. Words are used in a context. The context may be a bodily gesture, a tone of voice, a frown or a smile. We can limit our discussion to the consideration of words used in the context of other words, that is, in sentences.' This attitude was accepted by Couturat. It is a recognition of the practical limitation of all language but it does not necessarily prevent us from striving for the greatest possible monosignificance of the elements of the phrase. We need not argue, as some do, that because complete monosignificance is impossible to achieve we should reject the principle as a whole. In adopting roots the Ido Academy has defined their meaning in order to avoid a common danger to a planned language when used by different nationalities—the danger that each nation should attach the meaning of its ethnic equivalent to this root. Dyer's dictionaries (*Ido-English* and *English-Ido*, Pitman) give a great many of these definitions which are valuable to the student of Ido [*e.g.*, *asistar* = to be present, not to help; *aktuala* = present, up to-date, not actual as opposed to possible].

Jespersen comments on some problems of root selection in *I.L. and Science* which I quote here to show some of the difficulties which confronted the Ido Academy.

'Sometimes there exists a very troublesome rivalry between two words. In order to render the noun "arm" (limb) the proper word would seem to be the German, English, and Scandinavian "arm", until one makes the discovery that the same root "arm" in the sense of "weapon" is still more international [EFIS, supported by *armée* DEFR, *armata* I, *armada* S, *armieren* D, etc.] which compels us to have recourse for "arm" (limb) to a Romanic form. In other cases a more or less arbitrary change of one of the series of words appears to be the only means of avoiding confusing homonyms [namely, for door *pordo* instead of *porto*, on account of *port* = carry], but this procedure must be employed with great caution. Before everything else it is necessary to avoid all disguising of words, which makes them unrecognizable, aptly described by M Blondel as a masquerade. This masquerading was set up as a general principle in Volapük, though both Esperanto and Ido are by no means free from it, owing to their concessions to regularity.'

'As an example of the conflicts which occur now and then may be quoted the expressions for the idea of "soul". "Soul" is the word which would be immediately understood by the greatest number of people, but we cannot employ the English diphthong *ou*, as we must be very sparing in the use of diphthongs since they cause very great difficulties in pronunciation. We cannot take over the word in the form *sol*, because we require this for the word "alone" (IS *solo*, internationally used in music, E *sole*, F *seul*). D *Seele*, supported by the Scandinavian *själ*, is not familiar to a sufficient number of people, and, besides, we require the word *sel* for "saddle" (FIS). The French word *âme* will not do either, because it is not sufficiently well-known outside France, and, besides, there is a difficulty here too, for *am-* is absolutely required for the idea of "love" on account of FIS and many derivatives in E, not to mention the god Amor. The use of the Latin *anim-*, which is the basis of the Romanic forms, is impossible, since we cannot do without the adjectival termination *-al*, and *animal* would then mean partly "relating to the soul", partly "animal", which cannot be permitted in an international language. We must resort to the device of changing *anim-* a little, whereby we get *anmo*. This example will show how complicated the task frequently is of finding an international word which will give rise to no confusion or misunderstanding.'

If we compare the vocabulary of Ido with that of Esperanto we will find that Ido has adopted many international forms where Esperanto uses derivatives or compound forms which are less intelligible (Esp. *ek/kant/i* = Ido *inton/ar*; Esp. *de/centrifug/i* = Ido *centrifug/ar*; Esp. *ĉef-manĝo* = Ido *dine/o*; Esp. *meti/o-lernant/o* = Ido *aprentis/o*). Many more examples will be found in *Esperanto-Ido* (London, 1934).

The vocabulary of any language, national or international, is never complete. New terms are created through the development of science and industry, and it is more essential for a planned language to find agreement on the general principles of root selection than on separate words. The extension of the vocabulary for all branches of human activity will then be the task of a body of scientists and technicians who are thoroughly familiar with the problem, the principles agreed upon, and the requirements for these various terminologies.

II—5. An experiment in double translation

As a test of the precision of Ido, Louis Couturat translated a few paragraphs from *The Laws of Habit* by Professor William James (New York, H. Holt & Co., 1907) into Ido, which were then retranslated into English by P. D. Hugon without previous knowledge of the original. This short example shows that the planned language is capable of expressing and retaining the precise meaning of the original. The words of the retranslation are slightly different, but the meaning has remained identical with the original. I believe that most systems that are serious competitors for use as planned auxiliary languages are able to prove the same as Couturat has proved for Ido. This would confirm the general opinion among interlinguists that the problem of creating a planned language is no longer a question of the genius of a single inventor, but is simply the problem of coordinating the efforts of linguists and interlinguists on scientific lines.

Reference has already been made to the importance of vocabulary selection and an experiment, made with Ido, may briefly be mentioned. Vocabulary selection means the choice of the most important words for the purpose of teaching them as the first step towards the learning of the complete language, not a restriction or limitation of that language. The selected vocables should be the same in all countries to enable students to make use of them and profit by them on an international level from the very beginning.

The Teacher's Word Book by Thorndike, the Carnegie *Report on Vocabulary Selection* (King, London 1936), the *Semantic Frequency List* by Helen S. Eaton (University of Chicago Press) and other counts are valuable as a basis. The system by Palmer and Hornby *Thousand Word English* (Harrap, London 1937) has been translated into Ido (*Mil Vorti Ido*, London 1939). The authors divided all words into three groups, (1) names of species and things, (2) verbs or verbal roots, and (3) grammatical words. It was impossible to translate more than the primary and essential meanings of each word as otherwise we would have obtained a thousand-word list multiplied by all the possible significations of each word, that is an infinitely larger list than was wanted. Therefore a process of sifting was called for in which (*a*) all duplications of meanings, and (*b*) secondary meanings not part of the thousand most frequent terms were eliminated. Equally, compounds were divided into their component parts, and affixes were treated as countable units as they can be regularly combined with an almost unlimited number of verbal or substantival roots in Ido.

It was recognized that the difficulties of language learning are the difficulties of vocabulary rather than of grammar which can only be partially overcome by mnemonic aids. The deliberate reduction—as the first stage—can further minimize the effort in the use of a planned auxiliary.

THE LAWS OF HABIT

By Professor William James

(Original)

I believe that we are subject to the law of habit in consequence of the fact that we have bodies. The plasticity of the living matter of our nervous system, in short, is the reason why we do a thing with difficulty the first time, but soon do it more and more easily, and finally, with sufficient practice, do it semi-mechanically, or with hardly any consciousness at all. Our nervous systems have (in Dr Carpenter's words) *grown* to the way in which they have been exercised, just as a sheet of paper or a coat, once creased or folded, tends to fall for ever afterward into the same identical folds.

(From Talks to Teachers on Psychology, New York, H. Holt & Co.)

LA LEGI DI LA KUSTUMO

Traduko en Ido da L. Couturat

Me kredas, ke ni esas submisata a la lego di la kustumo per konsequo di la fakto, ke ni havas korpi. La plastikeso di la vivanta materio di nia nervala sistemo, esas, abrevite, la kauzo ke ni facas un kozo desfacile la unesma foyo, ma balde plu e plu facile, e fine, kun suficanta praktiko, ni facas ol mi-mekanike, o kun preske nula koncio. Nia nervala sistemi *kreskis* (segun la vorti di Dr Carpenter) en la voyo en qua li esas exercita, exakte quale folio di papero, o vesto unfoye faldita or shifonigita, tendencas falar sempre pose en la sama identa falduri.

(Some words and grammatical forms have been slightly adapted to conform to the decisions of the academy and the present usages of Ido.)

THE LAWS OF HABIT

Retranslated into English by P. D. Hugon

I believe that we are subject to the law of habit in consequence of the fact that we have bodies. The plasticity of the living material of our nervous system is, to put it briefly, the reason why we do a thing with difficulty the first time, but soon more and more easily, and finally, with sufficient practice, we do it half mechanically, or almost without any consciousness. Our nervous systems *have grown* (in Dr Carpenter's words) in the way in which they were trained, just as a sheet of paper or a garment, once folded or crumpled, tends to fall ever after in the same identical creases.

(The translator was unacquainted with the original before doing the retranslation.)

II—6. Comparative texts

(*The Emperor's New Clothes, by Hans Christian Andersen.*)
'Ho Deo!' il pensis, 'ka me esus stupida? Ton me nultempe kredis, e ton nulu darfas savar! Ke me ne esus apta por mea ofico? No, esus netolerebla, ke me dicas, ke me ne povas vidar la texuro!'
'Nu, vu ya dicas nulo pri to!' dicis unu del texisti.
'Ho, to esas belega! Tote charmiva!' dicis la olda ministro, regardante tra sua binoklo, 'ica desegnuro ed ica kolori! Yes, me dicos al imperiestro, ke ol plezas a me multege!'
'Nu, to joyigas ni!' dicis amba texisti, e li nomizis la kolori e la stranja desegnuro. La olda ministro askoltis atencoze, por ke il povez dicar lo sama pos retrovenir al imperiestro, e tale il agis.'
(*Comparative Texts, International Auxiliary Language Association* (*IALA*).)

(*A paragraph written by Louis de Beaufront* (*Kompleta Gramatiko di Ido.*)
La *Grammaire complète* quan ni publikigis prezente esas strikte konforma al decidi di la Komitato e dil Komisitaro Permananta; do ol ne plus esas, same kam la linguo ipsa, verko pure individuala; ol esas la final ed oficala rezultajo di la deliberi dil Komitato elektita reguloze dal *Delegitaro*, pos sep yari de propagado por l'ideo di linguo internaciona en la maxim diversa landi e medii.

(*A paragraph written by Louis Couturat, Progreso* 1909, *pp.* 580-681.)
Nur per la praktiko ni povas developar e perfektigar ol [the international language, Ed.]—(per la praktiko konciata, reflektata, lumizata e guidata da la kritiko e da la cienco).—Ti de nia amiki, qui fakte praktikas la linguo, savas, quale ni ipsa, ke to [system of grammar, derivation, and vocabulary, Ed.] esas nur skeleto o la framo di la linguo; la linguo ipsa konsistas en la frazifado (frazeologio)—on devas pensar en la linguo, do expresar *integra pensi* per idala frazi, qui havas, o povas havar, nula modelo en nia lingui. Or ta frazifado povas fixigesar nur *per* (ni ne dicas *da*) la praktiko, nam nur la praktiko rivelas la sennombra formi tradukenda, e pozas a ni, ye singla pazo, nova questioneti e problemeti. Pro to ni asertas tre sincere, ke nia linguo ne esas *facita*, ma *facata* e *facenda* konstante.

II—7. Commentary

The criticisms of Ido can be classified into several groups, (1) criticisms of principles (monosignificance, reversibility, logic), (2) criticisms of grammatical structure, (3) criticisms of word building elements, (4) criticisms of vocabulary. All four groups are closely connected, but it seems better to me, for the sake of clarity, to discuss the criticisms and suggestions for improvements for each division separately. A number of suggested improvements have been put forward by people with wide experience of the language. These discussions have taken place over a number of years in *Progreso, Mondo,*

La Akademio, La Muevi and other papers, and a synopsis can be found in Roze's *Raporto, decidi dil akademio interimal*, Part II, Riga, 1937.

(1) PRINCIPLES: A planned language should have all the characteristics of the ethnic languages; it should be flexible and should not contain any rigid elements which are not to be found in one or more of the European languages. The introduction of Couturat's logic into Ido is against the nature of language. Psychology plays a greater part in language than logic, 'language is not a product but a function' (W. Humboldt). Expression is a process of analogy rather than one of logical deduction. In Ido the application of logic has led to a certain amount of artificial rigidity. The principles of 'monosignificance' and 'reversibility' can only be achieved by adopting new roots, and word-building elements. Language lives and develops and the monosignificance of a certain term may disappear owing to a gradual extension of its meaning. The word 'radio' stood originally for something different from its present common use for 'wireless'. The strict application in Ido of the principle of 'reversibility' had to lead to the adoption of a large number of strictly defined affixes (-*aj*-, -*ur*-; -*if*-, -*iv*-, -*ig*-). Experience has proved that the correct use of either -*aj*- or -*ur*- and of other sets of affixes has proved difficult. Idists practising the language for many years have made repeated mistakes and in some cases the usage varies between different nationalities. The adoption of so many affixes must lead to a number of arbitrary selections which make the language rigid and artificial. The principle of logic, implying monosignificance and reversibility, is a principle selected *a priori* which condemns it in the opinion of interlinguists who adhere to the naturalistic school.

(2) GRAMMATICAL STRUCTURE: This problem is one of facility and internationality. The most common plural ending of the European languages is -*s*. Ido uses -*i* because -*s* is used for the convenient conjugational system of Ido [-*as* ,-*is*, -*os*]. This system has been taken over from Esperanto. The naturalistic languages adopted -*s* and -*es*, besides -*os* and -*as*. -*i* has the advantage of admitting of no exceptions or variations while the plural sign -*s* would have to be adopted with at least the addition of -*e* for nouns ending with a consonant. -*s* has the advantage of being more international but it introduces irregularities which should not be admitted for the sake of facility. A further structural criticism is that the planned language should have an analytic conjugation, *i.e.*, it should make use of a number of auxiliary verbs. The only auxiliary employed in Ido is *es*/*ar* which can be used analytically for the passive voice [*ilu esas punisata* = he is punished] or synthetically [*ilu punis*/*es*/*as*]. The naturalistic systems have a complete analytic conjugation. Janis Roze summarized some proposals (*Raporto*, Riga, 1937) for using the analytic conjugation in Ido. As a specimen he quotes Quarfood [*me did protektar; me vil protektar; me vud protektar; me hav protektita; me had protektita; me vil havar protektita; me vud havar protektita*].

(3) WORD BUILDING ELEMENTS: One of the main objections to Ido from the naturalists is the absence of the affix *-ation* which is to be found in the European languages. Jespersen said that this affix cannot be defined with one invariable meaning. Ido has not adopted *-ation* as an affix but has treated it as part of a number of roots spelt phonetically [*generacion/o*]. Jean Laurent has proposed *-aciono* as a new affix deriving the verbal noun [*doz/ar*, *doz/aciono*]. This proposal was widely discussed but has not been accepted. A precise and monosignificant definition cannot be given to it, and without such definition it would contravene the principles of monosignificance and reversibility.

The use of the suffixes *-if-* (to produce, secrete), *-ig-* (to make, render), and *-iz-* (supply with, furnish with) has met with difficulties in practical experience. They are correctly used only after considerable experience. To use *-ig-* correctly one constantly needs to know whether a certain verb is transitive or intransitive, and the dictionary must frequently be consulted. It is further said that outside the domains of science, where these suffixes are required for precision of expression, they should be reduced to their common *-i-* and be accepted as an agreed convention for direct derivation. *-ag-* = action with an instrument, should be similarly treated. The *-i-* would then only remain to indicate the omission of the full suffix, which should appear fully in scientific texts [*martel/i/ar* instead of *martel/ag/ar*, *petr/i/ar* instead of *petr/ig/ar*, *kron/i/ar* instead of *kron/iz/ar*]. This proposal has not been accepted.

The lack of direct derivation for substantival verbs [*shop, to shop; feather, to feather; hammer, to hammer*] is criticised by Esperantists and naturalists alike. Zamenhof in Esperanto, de Wahl in Occidental, and Jespersen in Novial have adopted this method, the two latter, however, with certain limitations. Ido has rejected such direct derivation as one is frequently uncertain in Ido whether a root is fundamentally a noun-root or a verbal root. The respective merits are more fully discussed in a separate chapter.

(4) VOCABULARY: We have seen that it is impossible to give an exact definition of the meaning of *-ation* and its variations (E *continue, continuation; consider, consideration; deliberate, deliberation*). Ido has consequently added this suffix to the root [*deviac/ar* = to deviate, *mediac/ar* = to mediate, *dominac/ar* = to dominate], but in a number of cases Ido has adopted two different roots for the same elemental meaning [*plantac/ar* = to plant, but *plant/o* = the plant; *embrac/ar* = to embrace, but *braki/o* = the arm; *poz/ar*, but *pozicion/o; formac/ar* = to form, but *form/o* = the form]. The contradiction in certain cases of internationality and monosignificance has led to the adoption of a second root which could not be derived from the first one [*potent/a, potenc/o, potencial/o; konces/ar, koncesion/ar*]. In cases where the regular derivative was formed, it no longer retained the internationally known form, owing to the fact that only one affix for one function could be admitted in Ido

[*inspekt/ist/o*], the known European form being a variation of inspector; *redakt/ist/o*, the European word being *redactor*; *explod/o* from *explod/ar*, the European forms being respectively explosion and to explode. Couturat said that if Ido would adopt *-aciono* it must also adopt *-iciono* and *-uciono* which would destroy the very principles of the language.

The two principles can be summarized as follows: (1) the naturalistic school formulates a set of rules of its flexional derivation which will allow the internationally known forms to be more or less regularly derived [*cede/r, cess/ion*], (2) the autonomistic school replaces the international words with compositions from monosignificant elements and introduces the international forms which it cannot regularly derive as new roots into the vocabulary [*poz/ar, pozicion/o*].

III. Occidental (1922) by Edgar de Wahl

III—1. History

EDGAR DE WAHL WAS born on 11th August 1867 in Olwiopol (Ukraine). He studied Volapük in 1887 and took up Esperanto a year later only to give it up again and to begin his independent studies in 1894. He turned his interest to a naturalistic solution of the problem and collaborated in 1906-7 with Rosenberger, the then president of the *Kadem bevünetik volapüka*, later the *Akademi Internasional de lingu universal*. In 1907 he submitted to the *Délégation pour l'adoption d'une langue auxiliaire internationale* a memorandum on the construction of an auxiliary language without submitting a complete language. The principal ideas in his memorandum were, (1) that none of the existing systems is satisfactory; (2) that the international language to be constructed, be founded on the international linguistic material; (3) that such project should have its own system of word formation, *i.e.*, really international words should be obtained through a number of rules formulated for that purpose; (4) that it should possess a grammar which produces no unnatural forms, *i.e.*, forms deviating from the ethnic languages; and (5) that it should possess an international orthography.

By 'natural' or 'international' de Wahl meant to describe those forms which are already known through various European languages. These ideas were not accepted by the *Délégation* to which they were submitted and de Wahl proceeded to elaborate his own system until, in 1922, he published them as his own language *Occidental*, in his paper *Kosmoglott*, later to be named *Cosmoglotta*. He restated his principles in a conversation with Jespersen in 1935 (*Novialiste*, No. 6) and required of an international language that each artificial language should respect the common laws of ethnic languages, *i.e.*: (1) It should be an organic, autonomous entity, living and growing according to its own laws, harmonizing and assimilating new elements, and not be a conglomeration of different words put together at random. (2) For our special purpose it should be based on the international forms common to the European languages in phonetics, spelling, and modes of expression.

To further its introduction it should also have the following qualities, (1) it should be comprehensible at first sight and without previous instruction to all civilized Europeans, (2) it should not shock the public through incomprehensible forms but should have the aspect of an almost natural language, and (3) to secure adoption and use it should not only be easy to read, but also easy for practical use, and easy in its grammatical structure.

Since 1922 the theories of de Wahl have attracted serious minds and have influenced Jespersen and his Novial to some extent. IALA (The International Auxiliary Language Association) has classified it as one of the systems of demonstrated usefulness.

III—2. Grammar

The *alphabet* comprises 26 letters, *y* fulfilling a double rôle as consonant and vowel. The vowels are *a* [pr. as in *father*], *e* [*fête*], *i* [*machine*], *o* [*most*], *u* [*rule*], *y* [F *u*, or D *ü*]. The 21 consonants are *b, c, d, f, g, h, j, k, l, m, n, p, r, s, t, v, w, x, y, z*. Several consonants have two pronunciations [*c* hard as 'k' before *a, o, u*, or any consonant; soft as 'ts' before *e, i, y*; *g* hard as in *gold* before *a, o, u*, or any consonant, soft as in *general* before *e, i, y*; *t* as 'ts' before *ie, ia, io*].

The *stress* falls on the vowel before the last consonant. The plural endings [-(*e*)*s*] and the adverbial endings [-*men*] are exceptions. Certain other grammatical endings [-*bil, -ic, -im, -ul, -um*] remain unstressed. Further exceptions not falling under any of these rules are marked with the accent [´, or `]. The length of the vowels varies. Unstressed syllables have the short vowel [*a* in *fan*, *e* in *bend*, *i* in *fit*, *o* in *drop*, *u* in *full*]. Stressed vowels followed by two consonants are short. The rest are long except in some short words, mainly prepositions.

Occidental has four diphthongs, *au, ay, ey, oy*, as well as *eu* in D *ö*.

The *definite article* is *li* for all genders and numbers. The *indefinite article* is *un*; *lu* may be used as an article if an adjective is used alone as an abstract conception.

The singular *noun* has no specific grammatical ending. The plural is formed by adding -*s* to words ending in vowels, or in -c, -g, -um; -*es* to words ending in other consonants. An exception, however, is -*e*, -*o*, -*a*, respectively used to distinguish neuter, masculine, and feminine [*camarad/e, /o, /a*].

The *pronouns* are *yo, tu, Vu, il, illa, it; noi, vu, ili*. The reflexive pronoun is *se*.

The *possessive pronouns* are *mi, tu(i), su; nor, vor, lor*.

The *verb* in the infinitive ends in -*r* [*ama/r*]. The present indicative is obtained by removing the infinitive ending [*yo ama, tu ama, il ama*].

The *imperative form* is the same as the present indicative, followed by a mark of exclamation [*!*]. The composite imperative is formed with *ples* plus the infinitive [*audi! ples audir*].

The *past tense* is obtained by adding -*t* to the present tense [*yo ama/t*].

The *future tense* is formed by employing the auxiliary *va* where English uses either 'shall' or 'will' [*yo va ear* = I shall go].

The *conditional* is formed by employing the auxiliary *vell* where English uses either 'should' or 'would' [*illa vell ear si yo vell consentir* = she would go if I should consent].

The *optative* is distinguished from the imperative by using *mey* with the infinitive [*que il mey trovar it* = that he may find it]. The *hortative* is formed with the word *lass* and the infinitive [*lass nos ear in li cité*].

Two *auxiliary verbs* are used, *ha/r* (an abbreviation of *have/r*), and *esse/r*, for the latter the abbreviated form *es* as an auxiliary and for the present tense.

The *perfect* and *pluperfect* tenses are formed by the auxiliary verbs preceding the past participle [*yo ha amat* = I have loved].

The *passive voice* is formed with the verb *esse/r* [*yo es vocat, yo es videt* = I am seen; *yo esset videt* = I was seen].

The *conjugation* of *esse/r* = *to be* is :

present tense	*past tense*	*future tense*
yo es (esse)	yo esset	yo va esser
tu (Vu) es	tu (Vu) esset	tu (Vu) va esser
il es	il esset	il va esser
illa (*or* ella) es	illa esset	illa va esser
it es	it esset	it va esser
noi es	noi esset	noi va esser
vu es	vu esset	vu va esser
ili es	ili esset	ili va esser

The *present participle* is *essent*; the *past* and *passive participle* is *esset*.

The *adjectives* are invariable in number and gender [*litt, bon, micri*].

The *adverbs* have no one grammatical ending. Some adjectives may be used as adverbs without alteration [*tó esset bon fat* = that was well done]. The adverbial endings -*men*, -*li*, -*ú* may be used, but a number of adverbs have no particular grammatical ending.

The *cardinal numbers* are: *un, du, tri, quar, quin, six, sett, ott, nin, deci, deci-ún* or *úndeci, deci-dú* or *dúdeci; duant* = 20, *triant, quarant; cent, ducent, sixcent*, etc.

The *ordinal numbers* are formed by the use of the suffix -*esim* [*unesim, duesim*, etc.].

The *degrees of comparison* are *bon, plu bon, max bon; bell, minu bell, minim bell*.

In *word derivation* Occidental accepts both the principle of direct and indirect derivation. Direct derivation is limited to certain cases which are indicated in the complete list of affixes below. For indirect derivation we must apply the three rules of de Wahl. To form nouns from verbal roots we detach the infinitive -*r* or -*e/r* [*vid, vid-e/r*] to obtain the perfect stem. RULE 1. If, after removing the grammatical ending [-r, -e/r] the stem ends in a vowel, add -t or change -y into -t [crea/r, crea/t, crea/t/or; atiny-e/r, atin/t, atin/t/ion]. RULE 2. If the final consonant of the stem should be either d or r, the letters are changed into -s [decide/r, deci/s, deci/s/ion]. RULE 3. In all other cases, except those especially cited below, the removal of the infinitive -r (or -er) gives the required perfect stem [duct/e/r, duct-, duct/ion]. The six exceptions are cede/r, perfect stem cess-; sede/r, sess-; move/r, mot-; tene/r, tent-; verte/r, vers-; veni/r, vent.

To form verbs from nouns and adjectives, we remove the endings and obtain the perfect stem. By adding -r or -er we will obtain, in most cases, the verb [decora/t/ion, decora/t, decora/r].

Syntax: The ordinary word order is subject-verb-object [li monument es plazzat avan li palazzo = the monument is (placed) in front of the palace]. Short adjectives generally precede the noun [un bon idé = a good idea]; long adjectives may follow the noun [li lingue international = the international language]. The interrogative phrase begins with esque [esque vu va promenar? = are you going to walk?] or any other interrogative pronoun or adverb [qui, quo, quande]. Inversion may be used without the interrogative esque [have vu li libre? = have you the book?]. The negation is indicated by the word ne [il ne ha fat it = he has not done it].

III—3. The affixes and their meaning

Certain prepositions may be used as affixes. They are not included in this list. The definitions of the meaning of the affixes and the examples are taken from an official Occidental publication. We shall have an opportunity to examine these meanings and the use of certain affixes in the commentary below.

PREFIXES

des- denotes contrary [des/facil]
dis- denotes in all directions [dis/tribuer]
in- denotes negation, not, un-, in-, ir- [in/util, in/regulari, in/possibil]; The preposition in- is sometimes used as a prefix but should not be confused with the prefix in- which latter is written with an accent for differentiation. The preposition is used with verbs [includer, invader].
mis- denotes wrong [mis/prender]
pre- denotes before [pre/judicie, pre/position, pre/ponderant]
re- denotes again [re/prender, re/form, re/stituer]
retro- denotes in an inverse direction [retro/spectiv, retro/ear]

SUFFIXES DENOTING PROFESSION

-ero, -era denotes business man, active person [labor/ero, barb/ero]
-ería denotes place of profession or business [vitr/ería, libr/ería = book shop]
-erie denotes business, profession, also goods sold or produced there [vitr/erie = glassware]. Also metaphorically features of character, way of acting frequentatively, diminutively, depreciatively [galant/erie, bigott/erie, diabol/erie]

PERSONAL MEANINGS

-ist   denotes a person occupied by, a spiritual, technical, or scientific subject often connected with an -ism [*social/ist, telegraph/ist, machin/ist*]

-és   denotes an inhabitant [*Angl/és, Franc/és, London/és*]. Many geographical references are, however, constructed with *-an*.

-ario   denotes person characterised by an external qualification or office [*million/ario, action/ario, secret/ario, comiss/ario*]

-on   denotes person characterised by root word, denoting the intrinsic quality of the root meaning [*gris/on* = E greyhead, *spi/on*]

-essa   denotes feminine dignity [*princ/essa*]

-ard   denotes a bad person [*furt/ard* = thief; *menti/ard* = liar]

SUFFIXES DENOTING QUALITIES

-ie   denotes abstract states, it may be added to the present participle of the verb to convert it into a noun [*malad/ie, existent/ie, audient/ie*]

-tá   denotes qualities, also as -(*i*)*tá* [*bon/*(*i*)*/tá, liber/tá, regular/*(*i*)*tá*]

-té   denotes collective totality [*homani/té* = humanity; *homani/tá* = human kindness; *majori/té*]

-ess   denotes personal qualities, states, conditions, situations [*yun/ess*]

-ore   in verbs denotes the state implied in the root word, taken in an active, forceful sense (see also *-ie*), affection, motion, or brightness, temperature [*am/ore, terr/ore, horr/ore, cal/ore, frig/ore*]; with adjectives a measurable condition [*long/ore, grand/ore, alt/ore*]

VERBAL SUFFIXES

-r   infinitive ending with added *-a-* [*-ar*] and used for direct derivation in the five following meanings :

    (1) with objects, materials, abstract matters to provide with [*arm/ar, sal/ar, privilegi/ar, motiv/ar*];

    (2) with instruments, showing their application [*scruv/ar, martell/ar, bross/ar*];

    (3) from nouns representing functional product or secretion of an organism, to separate it [*lact/ar, lacrim/ar, urin/ar, ov/ar, sangu/ar, saliv/ar*];

    (4) with persons in executive positions, in the exercise of their functions [*judic/ar, domin/ar*];

    (5) with adjectives and participles (mostly with prepositions *a-*, *in-*) to produce this quality (*plen/ar* = to fill, to fulfil; *sicc/ar* = to dry; *alontan/er* = to remove; *vivent/ar* = to revive]

-ear   infinitive ending, implying a dynamic condition, a moving, repeating, oscillating state, also state of brightness, temperature, and movement [*flamm/ear* = to be in flames; but *inflammar* = to set alight; *und/ear* = to be wavy; *flor/ear* = to be flowering; *verd/ear* = to be green]

-ettar   denotes continued action in a small way [*foli/ettar* = to run through the pages of a book]

-isar   denotes to make, in connection with adjectives and nouns [*ideal/isar, canal/isar real/isar, carbon/isar*]

-izar   of persons, denotes to act in the kind of [*tyrann/izar, mastr/izar,* = to master]

-ijar   denotes to become [*rub/ijar* from *rubi*, one *-i-* being suppressed; *verd/ijar* from *verd*(*i*)]

OTHER EXPRESSIVE SUFFIXES

-ach   denotes derogatory meaning [*dom* = house, *dom/ach* = hovel]

-astro   as in poetaster [*poet/astro, medic/astro* = quack]

-alya   collective nouns with the sense of disorder, something cast together, pell mell, a pack [*can/alya, antiqu/alya, ferr/alya*]

-ell   denotes young one [*leon/elles* = lion cubs]

-ade   denotes a fulness, series [*bocc/ade* = mouthful, from *bocca* = mouth; *manu/ade*]

-age   collective noun with the sense of order [*foli/age, bosc/age, plum/age*]; also something made of the root [*lact/age* = milk diet, *lan/age* = woollen material]

-agie   (with verbal roots) denotes activity, especially industrial one, the concrete result, metaphorically also place, time of it, the money which is to pay for it [*vi/agie*, from *via*, either the word ending -*a* or affix -*a* to be suppressed; *pass/agie* from *passa/r*, one -*a* to be suppressed; *miss/agie* = message from *misse/r*]

-atri   denotes like [*verd(i)-atri* = greenish, *spongi-atri* = spongy]

-atu   denotes a legal or other institution [*secretari/atu, celib/atu* = celibacy; *proletari/atu* = proletariat]

-al   denotes general relation [*nav/al* from *nave; fat/al* from *fate; mort/al* from the noun *morte* = death, not from the verb *mori/r* = to die which might form *mor(i)al*, or from *morta/r* = to kill; in all cases a vowel has to be suppressed]

-ic   denotes consisting of, being so, as internal quality [*electr/ic, hero/ic, epidem/ic*]

-bil   after consonants -*ibil*, derived from verbal roots (from perfect root if there is a special one), denotes possibility (*sta/bil* from *sta/r*; *vis/ibil* from *vide/r* (here the verbal root forms the noun according to de Wahl's rule, *d* = *s*, and the addition of the suffix will then result in the known word), *porta/bil* from *porta/r*]

-da   denotes a continued action [*cannon/a/da, fusil/a/da* from *fusil;* adding an -*a*- between the root and the suffix)]; -*e*- is changed to -*i*- before -*da* [*curri/da* = race from *curre/r* = to run; *lei/da* from *lee/r* = to read]; (we have met with cases where the -*e* has been suppressed after the infinitive ending -*r* has been taken away; here the -*e*- is not suppressed but changed into -*i*-)

-osi   denotes rich in [*numer/osi*]

-ment   denotes concretization of an action, the means by which, and for which an action is done [*orna/ment, funda/ment*] (the ending -*ion* denotes the action itself)

-ion   denotes action, states, and results [*destinat/ion, construct/ion, situat/ion, direct/ion, redact/ion*]

-ia   denotes place, especially geographical names [*Angl/ia, Franc/ia, German/ia, observator/ia, dormitor/ia* from *dormi/r*]

-ier-a   denotes a place containing [*carbon-iera* = coal mine; *torf/iera* = turf pit]

-ier-e   denotes a thing containing [*incr/iere* from *incre*]

-ier-o   denotes a holder [*candel/iero, pom/iero* (of fruit trees)]

NUMERAL SUFFIXES

-esim   to form ordinal numbers [*un/esim, du/esim, cent/esim*]

-esim   secondary meaning for forming fractions [*un six/esim*]

-plic   to form multiples [*du/plic, tri/plic*]

-en   to form collectives [*dec/en, quarant/en, cent/en*].

III—4. *Vocabulary*

The vocabulary is preferably based on the Romanic languages. De Wahl has preserved, wherever possible, the known international forms, and has adapted the rules of derivation for that purpose. Where no common root existed in the chief European languages, a word of Latin origin was chosen as the new root [E *eye*, F *œil*, D *Auge;* international words of Latin origin in E *ocular*, F *oculaire*, D *okular*], Occidental word *oculist, oculiste;* de Wahl has endeavoured to maintain the international forms of spelling wherever possible [*causa/r, curt, poc, senioretta, chambre, distinye/r, bote* = boat, *botte* = shoe]. In some cases double consonants may, or may not be used, the *Occidental-English Dictionary* (by Federn, Kemp, Haislund) gives both forms [*a(c)conosse/r, a(c)quisite/r, a(p)pere/r, a(t)tac(c)a/r*]. The principle of derivation modelled on the ethnic languages and historic spelling have **not**, however, always led to the known international word forms, as a look through the dictionary will show [*scrition, descovrition*].

III—5. *Comparative texts*

(*The Emperor's New Clothes, by Hans Christian Andersen*)

'Domine Deo!' il pensat, 'esque do yo es stult? To yo nequande ha pensat, e to null hom deve saver! Esque yo ne es habil por mi oficie? Ne, it vell esser insuportabil dir que yo ne vida li textage!'

'Nu, Vu ne dí necos pri it!' dit un del textores.

'O, it es bellissim! vermen charmant,' dit li old ministro e regardat tra su ocul-vitres, 'ti dessin e ti colores! Yes, yo va dir al imperator que it plese me mult!'

'Nu, to injoya nos!' dit ambi textores, e ili nominat li colores per lor nómin e li strangi dessine. Li old ministro escutat atentmen, por posser dir lu sam, quande il retrovenit al imperator, e talmen il fat.

(*Comparative Texts, International Auxiliary Language Association* (*IALA*).)

(*A text, written by the author, Edgar de Wahl* (*Cosmoglotta*, November 1938, *XVII*, 5).) Part of the article 'Pri li decisiones orto-grafic del francés academie.'

Si on fixa un ortografie, to deve esser fat secun un general e unitari principie, talmen, que chascun mey strax posser saver quel form usar. On posse comprender que che nos li absolut fix ortografie del Occidental ancor ne es introductet. Plures usa li tal nominat historic ortografie, altres desira un simplificat tal secun clar regules. Proque it ne es possibil postular de omni aprendentes qui ili mey conosser li latin etymologie, on deve certmen introducter un ortografie simplificat, quant possibil regulari, fonetic e etymologic (in regard de Occidental, naturalmen, e ne del Latin!). Pri ti problema nu labora nor academie, til que un vermen bon e unitari systema va esser elaborat, it recomenda se tolerar un libertá. On forsan reprocha a nor Occidental-Academie laborar tro lentmen. Ma noi lassa guidar nos del principie trovar li ver unitari metode, que vell satisfar tam li scientic e systematic postulationes quam li regularitá e unitaritá de procedenties. Noi ne desira far un tal decretiv e defectiv labor quam li Academie Francés. Pro to noi peti nor coidealistes have ancor patientie. . . .

III—6. *Commentary*

The most important characteristic of the structure of Occidental is the endeavour to obtain natural forms, *i.e.*, word forms identical to those of the great ethnic languages, and thus to secure immediate comprehensibility. The list of affixes of Occidental should be studied from that point of view. The rules of derivation and the variety of affixes formulated and selected by de Wahl serve to analyse existing forms rather than to derive autonomically new words from international roots and affixes. According to their definition, the suffixes *-ario, -ero (-a), -ist*, should be interchangeable in the sense of 'profession,' and we should be able to form *dent/ero* or *dent/ist*, and *secret/isto*, as the etymological origin is no longer common knowledge in the everyday use of the word. To avoid the pitfall of unfamiliar formations and the difficulty of synonymous suffixes, Ido and Novial have accepted a number of so-called international words in their complete form without deriving them [*sekretari/o*] and by using suffixes for one meaning only, *-ist* for occupation or profession [*dent/isto, labor/isto*]. This difficulty has been frankly admitted (Cosmoglotta 76) by de Wahl. He said that the majority of suffixes with their defined meaning do not exist in Occidental in order that anybody may compose new words for general use, but rather so that one may understand the meaning of derivatives used in our standard literature. The good examples of our writers should be followed. Jespersen remarks in *An International Language* (Allen & Unwin) that the much praised immediate comprehensibility of Occidental mainly applies to people who are already familiar with two or three of the great European languages. The autonomists (Esperantists and Idists) maintain the generally recognized principle that an auxiliary language should make the compulsory study of different ethnic languages superfluous and should be easy for those who know no other language but their mother-tongue.

According to its rules, Occidental uses the preposition *in* with the meaning 'in, into' as a prefix. The prefix *in-* indicates negation and is written, for the sake of differentiation, with the accent. Jespersen (*Int. Language*, p. 123) gives an example where both elements could easily be confused [*inscrit* = unwritten, *inscrit* = written in]. A prefix which leads to such confusion is a badly selected one, particularly if we consider that the ethnic languages have a variety of negative prefixes out of which a better one might have been chosen. A selection of English negative prefixes will prove the point: *mis-* as in *misunderstood, in-* as in *incomplete, un-* as in *unmistakable, im-* as in *impossible, il-* as in *illogical, ir-* as in *irregular, dis-* as in *distrust, de-* as in *decontrol, non-* as in *non-existent*.

The suffix *-tá* expresses quality, while *-té* expresses collective totality [*homan-i/té* = humanity; *homan-i/tá* = human kindness]. Clearly the definition 'quality' cannot express 'kindness' as well. Only usage has attributed this sense to the word 'humane'. To derive *homanitá* logically with a qualitative suffix and the root *hom-* does not lead to the meaning it is supposed to have. This view is confirmed if we examine another root [*soci/o* = fellow, member; *soci-e/té* = society; *soci-e/tá* = society, social structure].

CLASSIFICATION OF OCCIDENTAL

According to the theory of the brothers Friedrich and A. W. Schlegel, formulated in the early years of the last century, all languages are divided into three main types, *flexional*, *agglutinative*, and *isolating*. Flexional languages build their words from modifiable roots by the addition of intimately linked inflexions; agglutinative languages build them from invariable roots by means of invariable and monosignificant affixes, while those of the isolating type have no sort of formal grammatical structure. (For a more detailed description of these three types of languages see a later chapter.)

The isolating type of language does not use inflectional elements, and none of the planned languages of demonstrated usefulness (Esperanto, Esperanto-II, Ido, Occidental, Novial, Interlingua) is modelled on the isolating principle, but on either the flexional or the agglutinative type.

According to the flexional method of derivation, roots and affixes are modifiable both in spelling and meaning [Occidental : *vide/r* = to see; *vis-i/bil* = visible]. According to the agglutinative method, however, the roots are invariable in form and meaning and the affixes express an invariable relationship [Ido: *vid/ar* = to see; *vid/ebl/a* = visible].

De Wahl, the author of Occidental, unlike Zamenhof, de Beaufront-Couturat, and Jespersen, based his system on that of the flexional type of language, deriving his words from a common stem. Many words in Occidental are, however, derived according to the agglutinative method. In order to fit every flexional derivative into a regulated system, he formulated the following three rules :

RULE 1. If, after removing the grammatical ending [*-r*, *-e/r*] the stem ends in a vowel, add *-t* or change *-y* into *-t* [*crea/r*, *crea/t*, *crea/t/or*].

RULE 2. If the final consonant of the stem should be either *d* or *r*, the letter is changed to *s* [*decid/e/r*, *deci/s*, *deci/s/ion*].

RULE 3. In all other cases (barring six exceptions), the removal of the infinitive *-r* (or *-e/r*) gives the required perfect stem [*duct/e/r*, *duct-*, *duct/ion*].

Interlinguists have criticized the system of flexional derivation in Occidental for several reasons, (1) it contains a number of exceptions, (2) the meaning of roots and affixes are variable, *e.g.*, they are not monosignificant, (3) correct derivation in Occidental presupposes a knowledge of international words. I propose to examine each point separately.

The exceptions and irregularities: Occidental derives *vis/i/bil* from *vide/r*. According to rule 2 the removal of the infinitive ending *-r* leaves *vide-*, but here, as in many other cases, the *-e-* has to be suppressed although it is not a grammatical ending but part of the root. The letter *d-* is then transformed into *s-*. As the stem now ends in a consonant, *-i-* has to be inserted between stem and suffix, forming the derivative *vis-i/bil*. *-da* denotes 'continued action' and requires for some roots the insertion of *-a-* between stem and suffix [*cannon-a/da*], or the transformation of *-e-* into *-i-* [*curr-i/da*]. There are many similar cases. The suffix *-ion* denotes 'action, states and results'. It is added to the root *destruct-* after the removal of the infinitive *-r* and the suppression of the *-e*. In other cases it takes the form *-tion*, as in *constitue/r* = to constitute, *constitu/tion* = constitution. In *pass/agie*, derived from the verb *passa/r*, the root *-a* is suppressed; the Occidental grammar contains no rule to explain this exception. Six regular exceptions are admitted and many others should be added to this list.

The meaning of roots and affixes : *-or* denotes, according to Federn (*Grundlage für einen Terminologischen Code*, 1936) 'active agent', also 'machines' [*redact/or, compress/or, mot/or, isolat/or*]; the word *dormit/or/ia* = dormitory is derived from *dormi/r*, but *-or* in this case means neither 'active agent' nor 'machines' and its derivation cannot be logically justified.

In his conversation with Jespersen, de Wahl admitted the difficulty of defining the meaning of suffixes (*Novialiste*, No. 6, 1935). He said that it is true that several suffixes have a similar meaning which is not precisely defined but that the majority of these different forms can be found not only in the Romanic and Germanic languages, but also in Russian and Estonian. De Wahl further says that the suffixes of Occidental are not strictly obligatory as in other planned languages, but are to be taken preferably as an explanation and a model. The reason is, that the majority of people use analogy rather than logic. Thus, according to de Wahl, logic cannot be strictly applied to an elastic medium of communication.

The suffix *-erie* is a good example, for it is defined as denoting 'business, profession', also 'goods sold or produced at a place', 'features of character, way of acting frequentatively, diminutively, depreciatingly'. It follows that a planned language which aspires to complete naturalness cannot attribute one invariable meaning to its affixes if it admits the complete words of the ethnic languages.

Knowledge of international word forms: The rules of derivation in Occidental determine, though imperfectly, the forms of the words, but seldom their exact meaning. Occidental does depart, in fact, from the principle of the complete international word. A word is analysed and its elements defined accordingly; it is not derived autonomously from monosignificant word-building material. The meaning of an affix may have extended through usage and development. In the European languages this is not detrimental to learning as the word particle is no longer felt to be an affix but is learned as part of a complete word. In Occidental, however, it has again been detached from the full international word and has been defined as an affix. As the affix has now to fulfil the function of explaining the complete words in the European languages, its definition necessarily becomes loose and less precise. It would be difficult to analyse correctly the Occidental words *destination, construction, direction, redaction* by saying that the affix *-ion* (or its variations *-tion, -ation*) denotes 'action, states', or 'results.' A few further examples from English may show the difficulty of defining *-ion* [*-tion, -ation*]: [E *civilize, civilization; combine, combination; rotate, rotation; qualify, qualification, delegate, delegation*]. The conclusion is that, to use Occidental correctly, a fairly wide knowledge of the international words of the European languages is required—a demand which should not be made of people who wish to use a planned auxiliary language—which should be 'easiest for the greatest number of people.'

PLEONASTIC ENDINGS

In interlinguistics the term *pleonastic endings* has been used to describe specific grammatical terminations. In the opinion of some critics, these grammatical terminations are superfluous [*-o, -i, -a, -e*, etc.].

To what extent are specific grammatical terminations pleonastic? Ido and Esperanto use these endings to indicate the grammatical class to which a word belongs [*dom/o* = house = noun; *bel/a* = beautiful = adjective; *rapid/e* = rapidly = adverb, etc.]. These endings help the student to recognize a given text more easily; they fulfil a similar function to the use of differentiating colours in electrical wiring. As these terminations do fulfil this function, they cannot, correctly, be described as superfluous. Whether such function is desirable from the critic's point of view may be decided at a later date. For the purpose of interlinguistic discussion the term pleonastic is incorrect, or at least highly tendentious, if applied to either the Esperanto or Ido denotative terminations.

Occidental, Novial, and Interlingua, the systems of the naturalistic school, use definite grammatical terminations only in certain cases. In Occidental a word may, or may not have a final *-e* [*hom(e)*, *menti(e)*, *fat(e)*] which may, or may not be suppressed if a suffix is added to the word, and further the *-e* does not fulfil a grammatical function, for it is optional and many nouns do not end in *-e* [*dom, dessin, parol, regul*]. This irregularity may even apply to the same root [*soci/o* = fellow, member, pleonastic ending *-o*]; in combination with the suffix *-tá* or *-té*, the ending *-o* changes into *-e* [*soci-e/tá* = society, social structure, *soci-e/té* = society, club].

The conclusion then is that the regular grammatical terminations of Esperanto and Ido fulfil the function of classifying words as *nouns adjectives, adverbs,* etc. while Occidental admits optional endings which have no grammatical function.

A nonlinguist who is studying a planned language might well find it easier to recognize a word by its grammatical ending than to classify it as a *noun, adjective,* or *adverb* by memorizing its translation. Either method will give good results if correctly applied, but for the purpose of the planned language, the easier method will be the better one.

IV. Novial (1928) by Otto Jespersen

IV—1. History

OTTO JESPERSEN (1860-1943), a member of the Royal Danish Academy of Sciences, for many years lecturer at London University, the University of Copenhagen and author of many works on linguistics, was one of the few professional linguists who took an early interest in the movement for a constructed artificial language. He wrote his first article on the question in January 1904 for *Englische Studien* on the suitability of English as an international language. After having rejected Volapük as impossible and after studying the far superior Esperanto, Jespersen became closely associated with the *Délégation pour l'adoption d'une langue auxiliaire*. He was a member of its permanent commission and was later elected president of the Ido Academy, a position he held from 1907 to 1910. For some time he remained an active member of that academy and wrote the *History of Our Language* (Ido). In 1918 he contributed the preface to the *Ido-Deutsch* dictionary by Feder and Schneeberger in which he formulated the maxim, 'that international language is best which in every point offers the greatest facility to the greatest number,' which he modelled on Hutcheson's and Bentham's famous dictum, 'That action is best which accomplishes the greatest happiness for the greatest number.' He enlarged upon that principle by saying that it does not mean, as some would have it, that we should take Chinese as our interlanguage, for the simple reason that it is known to the greatest number of men. The principle does not apply, as he made clear on several occasions, to an absolute number of people, but only to the number of those people who require communication with other nations. But the facility which he demands is not merely a superficial facility by which a printed message can be understood at first sight—that is something, but not everything. An auxiliary language, to be useful, must be easy not only for the reader, but also for the writer and the speaker. An irregularly formed word may be easy of comprehension to anyone who has it in his own language or who knows it from another language with which he happens to be familiar, but at the same time, it may be very difficult to anybody else, much more difficult than a regular formation employing a suffix he has learnt once for all and which can be applied to a number of

72

words. Jespersen thus aspires to the greatest possible regularity—admitting of some small exceptions, well motivated and easily remembered—saying that no constructed language is totally exempt from exceptions. He further demands simplicity in structure and economy in its derivative elements. What we already know is something easy, and because he wishes to create a language to be used by many different nations, it is essential to find words and forms already known to the greatest number of people. Elements which are already in part or wholly international should form the main basis of that language. This leads him to demand naturalness without ignoring the fact that not all forms appear equally natural to all nations. The language must be able to express clearly and with precision the thoughts of modern man.

After extensive experience in the field of international language, Jespersen published his own system in 1928 and called it the *New International Auxiliary Language* (*Nov IAL* = *Novial*). The former Ido journal *Mondo* (Stockholm), renamed *Novialiste* since 1934, served as the organ of linguistic discussion for the group of people who considered it a better system than others previously published.

IV—2. Grammar

The *alphabet* comprises 23 letters. The vowels are *a* [pr. as in *father*], *e* [*fête, yes*], *i* [*machine*], *o* [*most*], *u* [*rule*]. The 18 consonants are *b, d, f, g, h, j* [as in *journal*], *k, l, m, n, p, q(u), r, s, t, v, x, y* [pr. as in *yes*]. While *c* is not admitted as a single consonant, it appears in the digraph *ch* admitted with the same value as the digraph *sh*. *c* and *z* have been abolished for ordinary dictionary use but are admitted for proper names and for abbreviations of chemical elements. Double consonants to differentiate the meaning of words [D *biete, bitte*] are not admitted.

The *stress* falls on the vowel preceding the last consonant. The addition of the ordinary consonant endings does not change the stress of the main word.

The *definite article* is *li* for all genders and numbers. The indefinite article is *un*.

The *singular noun* has no determinative grammatical ending. The plural is formed by adding -*s*. The grammatical endings are respectively used to indicate persons, no sex indication or distinction [-*e*], masculine [-*o*], and feminine [-*a*] [*home, homes; homo, homos; homa, homas; nule* = no one, *nulo* = no man, *nula* = no woman].

A special neuter ending -*um* has been introduced [*li bonum de ti situatione es ke . .* = what is good in that situation is that . . .]. The neuter plural is formed in -*um/es* or -*us* [*ver/um/es* = true things, or *ver/us*].

The *personal pronouns* are *me, vu, le, lo, la*, for things *lu; nus, vus, les, los, las; lus* for things. The reflexive pronoun is *se*.

The *possessive pronouns* are *men, vun, len, lon, lan; nusen, vusen, lesen, losen, lasen*.

The *verb* in the infinitive has no definite grammatical ending (*ama, protekte, mari, konstitu*] but the English to = *tu* has been introduced to indicate the infinitive.

The *present tense* is expressed by the stem [*me ama vu, lo protekte nus*].

The *imperative* is indicated by the simple stem [*Veni!*].

The *hortative* is indicated by *let* [*let nus starta, let on pensa kom on vol!*]. The *optative* is indicated by *mey* [*mey lo viva longitem!*].

The *past tense* is obtained by adding -*d*, or -*ed* if the stem ends in a consonant [*ama/d, protekte/d, mari/d, es/ed*].

The past can also be expressed by an analytic form for which Jespersen introduced *did* [*me did ama, lo did estima la*].

The *future tense* is formed by employing *sal*, from English shall, but this has later been changed to *ve*, but often the simple present may be used to express futurity, if there is some time indication like 'to-morrow', in the sentence [*me joya tu sal visita vus*], or the newer form [*tu ve visita vus*].

The *conditional* is formed by employing the auxiliary *vud* [*se lo vud veni, me vud rida* = if he came (should come) I should laugh].

The *perfect* and *pluperfect tenses* are formed with the auxiliary *ha* and *had* in combination with the infinitive verb form, not the participle [*me ha perda klefe* = I have lost a key, *me had perda klefe* = I had lost a key]. *Ha* and *had* must be used with all verbs, even in cases where some ethnic languages use 'to be' [*lo ha veni* = er ist gekommen].

These auxiliaries can be combined [*vu sal ha perda* = you will have lost, *la vud ha veni* = she would have come].

The *present participle* is formed by adding -*nt* to the infinitive [*hant veni* = having come]; the past or passive participle is formed by adding -*t* to the infinitive.

The *passive voice* is formed with the auxiliary 'to be', *bli* [preterite *blid*] for the passive of becoming, combined with the stem-form of the verb. The passive of being (expressing the state of) is expressed by *es* and the passive participle [*lon libres blid venda in grandi nombre* = his books were sold in great numbers; *li libre es vendat* = the book is sold]. With verbs like hate, praise, blame, admire, see, hear, Jespersen admits equally *bli* or *es* because these verbs denote an activity that is not begun in order to be finished.

The chief parts of the *verbal system* of Novial are:

active	passive
me protekte	me bli protekte
me protekted (did protekte)	me blid protekte
me ha protekte	me ha bli protekte
me had protekte	me had bli protekte
me sal protekte	me sal bli protekte
me sal ha protekte	me sal ha bli protekte
me vud protekte	me vud bli protekte
me vud ha protekte	me vud ha bli protekte

The *adjectives* are invariable in number and gender [*natural formes*]. For euphony Jespersen adds an *-i* to the adjectives saying that it is optional, admitting thereby alternative forms [*bon, boni, kruel, krueli, matur, maturi, sam, sami, publik, publiki*]. If the adjective is used by itself with reference to a noun just mentioned (anaphorically) a plural *-s* may be added to the *-i* which is then obligatory [*Hir es multi roses, ob vu prefera li blankis o li redis?* = here are many roses, do you prefer the white or the red ones ?].

The *cardinal numbers* are: *un* or *uni, du, tri, quar, sink, six, sep, ok, nin, dek, sent, mil*. For the tens is added the suffix *-anti* [20 = *duanti*, 30 = *trianti*; *quaranti, sinkanti, sixanti, sepanti, okanti, ninanti;* 23 = *duanti tri*, 99 = *ninanti nin*]. Nouns may be formed in *-o* [*duo, trio*, etc.]. Jespersen does not expect that ambiguity will arise out of such use, although *-o* is used to express the masculine.

The *ordinal numbers* are formed by the use of the suffix *-esmi* [*unesmi, du-esmi, sent-esmi*; 345th = *trisent-quaranti-sink-esmi*]; adverbs can be formed by *-im* [*unesm-im* = firstly].

The *degrees of comparison* are *bon(i), plu bon(i), maxim bon(i); bon(i) min bon(i), minim bon(i)*.

Syntax: The ordinary word order is subject-verb-object. The interrogative phrase begins with *qui* or one of its inflected forms *que* [*quo, qua*], *quum* [*Pro quum* = why]; *ob* is used in phrases like *Ob tum non fita belisim?* = Does this not fit beautifully? The negation is indicated by *no*.

IV—3. The affixes and their meaning

Certain prepositions may be used as prefixes.

PREFIXES

pre-	denotes before [*pre/vida* = foresee, *pre/historie, pre/paga*]
anti-	denotes against, chiefly in technical words [*anti/alkoholisme, anti/militariste*]
non-	negative prefix, being the adverb for 'not' [*non/existent, non/posibli, non/real*]
des-	denotes the direct opposite [*des/agreabli, des/avantaje, des/aproba*]
dis-	denotes dispersion or separation [*dis/dona* = distribute, *dis/trancha* = carve; but *disolu* = dissolve, instead of the regular formation *dis/solu*]
mis-	used with verbs denotes wrongly [*mis/pronuntia, mis/dukte, mis/komprenda, mis/kalkula*]
mal-	corresponds to the adjective *mal(i)* = bad, and the adverb *malim* = badly [*mal/odoro, mal/humurosi, mal/famosi* = ill-famed]
par-	denotes perfect or thorough action [*par/lerna* = to learn thoroughly, *par/lekte*]
ri-	denotes repetition or restoration [*ri/elekte, ri/skripte*]
retro-	denotes back(wards), inverse action [*retro/ira, retro/dukte, retro/seda* = cede back, restore]
mi-	denotes half [*mi/hore, mi/klosat* = half closed, *mi/lume* = twilight]

bo- denotes relation by marriage [*bo/patro* = father-in-law, *bo/filia*]
ex- denotes late, former, retired [*ex/rego, ex/profesoro*]
arki- corresponds to arch- [*arki/episkopo, arki/anjele*]
pseudo- from Greek with its international meaning [*pseudo/profeto, pseudo/filosofo, pseudo/sientali*]

SUBSTANTIVAL SUFFIXES

-o denotes nouns immediately derived from or connected with a verb. They mean the simple act or state denoted by the verb and are called by Jespersen the *nexus-substantives*. Jespersen deals at some length with the question of direct or immediate derivation which this ending *-o* covers for many different cases. I shall have to give many of his examples to make his solution of the intricate question of direct derviation perfectly clear.

The verb may end in *-a* and we get the *-a/o* words, for example *marcha/o, promena/o, komensa/o, odora/o, separa/o*. Or we have verbs ending in *-e* and we get the *-e/o* words, for example *respekte/o, introdukte/o, diskuse/o, opine/o* = think, have an opinion. In these two cases the final vowel is replaced when we form the verbal noun [*march/o, opin/o*]. If the verb ends in either *-i* or *-u*, the final vowel remains. Thus we have the *-i/io* words and the *-u/uo* words, for example, *aboli* = to abolish, *aboli/o* = the act of abolishing, *puni/io, nutri/io, defini/io, expedi/io, dormi/io; distribu/uo, kontribu/uo, evolu/uo, intervu/uo, diminu/uo*.

The cases in which Jespersen departs from the noun, ending in *-e* are more complicated. The verb directly derived from it ends in *-a*, and the verbal noun derived from the latter ends in *-o*. This is the *-e/a/o* class of words. The original noun means an instrument, and the verb denotes 'the natural use of the instrument' [*bros/e* = brush, *bros/a* = to brush, *bros/o* = the act of brushing ('my hat wants a brush'), *telefon/e, telefon/a, telefon/o, bisikl/e, bisikl/a, bisikl/o; fum/e* = smoke, *fum/a* = to smoke, *fum/o* = the act of smoking, *grup/e/a/o, plas/e/a/o, argument/e/a/o plant/e/a/o; dans/e* = dance, *dans/a* = to dance, *dans/o* = the action of dancing; *vot/e/a/o* = a vote, to vote, voting; *niv/e/a/o* = snow, to snow, the act of snowing; *sang/e/a/o* = blood, to bleed, bleeding]. Jespersen says that there is no conflict between using these grammatical endings *e/a/o* to denote respectively 'the instrument or thing', 'the action to which it is naturally applied', and the verbal noun expressing the 'state of action', and the use of *e/a/o* to denote neuter, male, and female in the case of living beings, for the two classes of words are easily kept apart by their natural meanings and no occasion arises to derive words in *-a* immediately from words denoting living beings.

Direct derivation should be admitted, says Jespersen, only in cases where there is not the slightest doubt as to the meaning of the verb thus created. He instances several cases where direct derivation would lead to misunderstanding. Their meaning is only fixed by usage and convention and may vary in different ethnic languages [E *to stone* = to kill by means of stones, or to separate fruit from stones; D *ochsen* = to work like an ox, but *kalben* = to calve].

-isa   denotes to provide with [*arm/isa*]

-eso   to form abstracts, denotes the state of being [*ver/eso* = the fact of being true, but *verum* = truth; *rich/eso, febl/eso, util/eso, blind/eso*]. This suffix may be added to a passive participle [*li venkat/eso de Napoleon da Wellington*, or *li venko de Wellington super Napoleon*].

-ione   denotes partly the result (as a whole) or the resulting state, partly the way or manner in which something is done, they may take either of the forms

                           -atione if the verb ends in -a,
                           -itione if the verb ends in -i,
                           -utione if the verb ends in -u.

            [*komunik/atione, instit/utione, defin/itione*]. Jespersen explains the -*t* by saying that -*ione* is added to the passive participle of all verbs except those ending in -e [*opin/e, opin/ione; diskus/e, dis-kus/ione; satisfakt/e, satisfakt/ione*]. While verbs ending in either -*a*, -*i*, or -*u* retain their ending and add -*t* before -*ione*, the verbs ending in -e lose their ending and do not add -*t*. As in Ido, some words in -*ione* are taken as new complete roots into the diction-ary without being derived from a corresponding verb [*okasione, emotione, sektione, funktione*].

-um   denotes the product of action (as distinct from the way in which it is done) to be added to the passive participle [*fabrikat/um* = manufactured article; *kreat/um; printat/um* = printed matter; *kopiat/um* = a thing copied].

-ure   denotes the result or product (as dinstinct from the act itself) *pikt/ure, skulpt/ure, invent/ure, fotograf/ure* = photo, while the thing photographed is *fotografat/um*]

-ere, or -iste denotes operator or person occupied with [*telegraf/ere, tele-graf/iste (-o, -a), bak/ere*]. The suffix is also used for animals and certain plants [*rept/ere, rod/ere, klim/ere*]

-iste   exclusively used for human beings, denotes adherents of a doctrine [*ate/iste, sosial/iste, monark/iste*], or for those occupied in certain professions or sciences [*art/iste, dent/iste, okul/iste, logik/iste, sient/iste, spesial/iste*]; -*iste* and -*ere* may be used to in-dicate respectively a professional man and an amateur, but this distinction is not carried through, and in some cases the two suffixes may be used indiscriminately.

-isme   denotes doctrine [*ate/isme, sosial/isme*]

-iere   denotes a person or thing characterized by a certain object or considered as its bearer [*rent/iere, pom/iere* = apple tree, *kandel/ iere, milion/iere*]

-arie   denotes recipient of an action, the person for whom something is destined [*send/arie* = addressee, *pag/arie* = payee]

-ilo   denotes a tool or instrument for doing what is indicated by a verb [*skript/ilo* = any kind of writing instrument, *lud/ilo* = play-thing, *orn/ilo* = ornament]

-ia   denotes the domain, province or country of someone [*Angl/ia* = England, *Frans/ia; duk/ia*]. Also applied to the spiritual domain [*filosof/e, filosof/ia, astronom/ia; printer/e* = printer, *printer/ia* = printing office]

-torie   denotes place where something is done [*labora/torie, observa/ torie, dormi/torie*]

-aje   denotes something made of, consisting of, having the character of [*lan/aje* = woollen goods, *lign/aje, plant/aje, kruel/aje*]

-ede   denotes quantity which fills something [*kulier/ede, manu/ede* = handful, *bok/ede* = mouthful]

-aro   denotes a collection, group, set of things or persons [*hom/aro, vort/aro* = vocabulary, *libr/aro*]

-ide   denotes descendant [*Pele/ide, Napoleon/ide, Herakl/ide*]

-yune   denotes young one [*bov/yune, han/yune, kat/yune*]

VERBAL SUFFIXES

-ira   denotes living beings acting as . . . [*profet/ira* = prophesy, *interpret/ira, rival/ira, rebel/ira*]

-isa and *-ifika* denotes to make into, transform into, render [*real-i/sa, ideal-i/sa, just-i/fika, rekt-i/fika*]. For both suffixes the preceeding *-i* may be taken as the adjective ending, the real suffix then being *-sa* and *-fika*. Both affixes may be used alternatively if the speaker does not remember or does not know the original ethnic form. Jespersen admits an exception for the verb *elektr-i/sa*, meaning to charge with electricity, and *elektr-i/fika* to electrify a railway. He also admits the ending *fika* as a new autonomous root with the meaning to render, make into, make [*lo fika li kavale kurse* = he makes the horse run]; *-isa* is also used to denote to provide or supply with, cover with [*arm/isa* = to arm, *harmon/isa, orient/isa*]

-ad-   denotes repeated or continuous act [*frap/ado* = continued beating]

-eska   denotes the beginning of an action or state [*dormi/eska, vid/eska, kurs/eska, am/eska, pal/eska, old/eska*]

ADJECTIVAL SUFFIXES

-al   denotes relating to; before this suffix the ending of the noun disappears except *-u* which is retained [*univers/al, nation/al, tradition/al; manu/al, sexu/al*]

-an   denotes inhabiting or belonging to a class or party [*Itali/an, Amerik/an, urb/an, akademi/an, senat/an, partis/an*]

-ari   denotes agreeing with, or fit for [*regl/ari, popul/ari, revolution/ari, element/ari, ordin/ari*]

-osi   denotes possessing or having, especially having in great quantity, full of [*por/osi, kuraj/osi, danjer/osi, misteri/osi*]. The optional adjectival ending *-i* should be retained when this suffix is used, as otherwise it might be taken for the plural of *-o*.

-isi   with adverb *-isim* denotes a very high degree [*grand/isi* = enormous, *grand/isim* = enormously, *bel/isi, bel/isim, varm/isi*]

-iv (-ivi) denotes doing naturally, or capable of doing [*instrukt/e, instrukt/iv(i), sugest/iv, atrakt/iv, akt/iv*]

-asi   denotes having the tendency or inclination to . . . [*mord/asi, disput/asi, labor/asi, atak/asi*]

-bli   denotes passive possibility [*lekt/e, lekte/bli, explika, explika/bli, audi, audi/bli*]; it always retains the vowel-ending of the verb.

-endi   denotes that must be, and *-indi* that deserves to be [*lekt/endi* = that must be read, *lekt/indi* = that is worth reading, *am/indi, solu/endi, solu/indi, expedi/endi*]. Before both affixes the verbal endings *-u* or *-i* must remain, but the endings *-a* or *-e* disappear.

GENERAL SUFFIXES

-et-	diminutive suffix [*river/ete* = brook, *urb/ete* = small town, *libr/ete*]. Also for terms of affection [*patr/eto, matr/eta*].
-on-	denotes greatness, quantity [*pluv-ono* = heavy rain]
-ach-	denotes contempt [*kaval/acha, jurnal/ache, kant/acha, kri/acha*]

NUMERAL AFFIXES

-anti-	to form tens [*du/anti* = 20, *tri/anti, ok/anti*]
-o	to form nouns from numerals [*du/o, tri/o*]
-esmi	to form ordinal numbers [*un/esmi, sent/esmi*], adverbs are formed by adding -*m* [*un/esmi/m* = firstly]
-ime	to form fractions [*sent/ime* = 100th part, *sink six/imes* = five sixths]
-opli(m)	multiplying suffix [*du/opli*]
-opim	distributive adverbs [*tri/opim* = in threes]

ADVERBIAL SUFFIXES

A number of abbreviated nouns are used as adverbial suffixes; they are given here in their abbreviated form.

-tem	(from *temp*) denotes time [*nul/tem* = never, *altri/tem*]
-foy	denotes time in repetition [*du/foy* = twice, *altri/foy, chaki/foy*]
-lok	denotes place [*omni/lok, nuli/lok, altri/lok*]
-kas	(from *kasu*) case [*omni/kas* = in every case, *irgi/kas* = anyway]
-grad	denotes degree [*alti/grad, kelki/grad*]
-man	(from *manere*) manner [*omni/man* = in every way, *altri/man*] When manner is not expressly denoted, this -*man* may be further shortened into -*m* [*privati/m, separati/m, spesiali/m, nuli/m, angli/m* = in English]

IV—4. Vocabulary

The roots of Novial are selected according to the principle of greatest internationality. In certain cases Jespersen prefers Germanic roots where both Ido and Occidental have chosen Romanic roots [*klema* from D *klemmen, pressen;* *vud* from E *would; even* as in English]. The main differences between the Novial vocabulary and those of the other systems come from the suppression of the letters *c* and *z*. The letter *s* plays an important part but tends to distort some words [*sientie* = science, *sesa* = F cesser, *sivil(i)* = civil]. But Jespersen has, as in Ido, retained the chemical formulæ and the well-known abbreviations of measurements. The total vocabulary adopted contains approximately 5,600 roots. A linguistic body could develop this vocabulary as the need arises, and on the principles laid down by Jespersen or accepted by him from other systems. In *An International Language* he points out a few words which might be taken as derivatives but in fact are complete words, *prob(-)abli*, meaning probable; but might be taken as meaning that which can be tested; *pos(-)ibli* = possible, not that which can be placed, *seri(-)osi* = serious, not full of series, *romane* = Roman, not novel, *rid(-)ono* = giving again, not laugh, *par(-)dona* = pardon, not give fully, *par(-)fuma* = perfume, not smoke thoroughly.

In his *Lexike* (Allen & Unwin) he admitted a number of alternative forms [*dogma, dogmate, sele, selule*] and in *Novialiste* 1, 1934, he published 49 words which were either omitted or which represent alternative forms considered preferable to those originally proposed.

One outstanding observation equally applies to all systems and should be mentioned here, that is, the agreement among all authors and interlinguists on the general principles of root-selection, the greatest internationality compatible with the particular grammatical structure of the system concerned. A careful study of the vocabularies of the four main systems, Esperanto, Ido, Occidental, Novial, will prove that some thousand words are the common property of these planned languages of demonstrated usefulness.

IV—5. *Comparative texts*

(*The Emperor's New Clothes, by Hans Christian Andersen.*)

(Written in the original Novial form as in *An International Language* (Allen & Unwin), a version in the new form will be quoted from the IALA Comparative Texts after the subsequent changes in Novial have been discussed in the following section.)

'Men Deo!' lo pensad, 'ob es posibli ke me es stupid? Tum me ha nulitem opine, e tum nuli home darfe sava! Ob me non es habil por men ofisie? No, vud es non-tolerabli ke me nara ke me non vida li texatum.'

'Nu, vu dikte nulum pri lum!' dikted un ek li texeres.

'O, lum es belisi! totim charmivi!' dikted li oldi ministro, regardant tra sen lunetes, 'dis desine e dis kolores! Yes, me sal dikte al emperere ke lum plesa me tre multim.'

'Nu, tum plesira nus!' dikted li du texeres, e li nomad li kolores e li stranji desine. Li oldi ministro auskultad atentim, por tu pove dikte li samum, kand lo venid retro al emperere, e talim lo fad.

(*A text written by the author, Otto Jespersen. Novialiste* 1, 1934, '*Plubonisat novial.*')

Me voli fa hir un konfesione: durant li lasti du o tri yares me ha okupa me primim pri tri grandi libres pri anglum e general linguistike, kel me volid ante omnum fina; me ha dunke have tre poki tempe tu pensa pri novial e tu responda letres pris dis lingue. Kand me ri-komensad skripte in e pri novial, me deskrovad ke me had oblive multum, ma kom rekompenso me nun pove vida men propri kreatum quasi fro distantia, quasi kom novi kose non-dependanti de me, e pove in konsekuo judika pri detales non-partisanim. Me ha anke reflekte multim pri li deklaratione del tri linguisti profesores kel asistad li konfero de IALA in Genève in 1930 (Debrunner, Funke, Hermann); les pronuntia kontre li tro grandi tendentie de kelki interlinguistes tu introdukte subtil distinktiones en konstruktet lingues. On ve vida in li sekuentum efektes de omni disum.

IV—6. Subsequent changes in Novial

In 1934 Otto Jespersen introduced certain changes in Novial which he admitted besides the original forms, saying that experience and experiment should show which are the better.

As a preferable alternative he introduces *ve* besides *sal*, and *ved* besides *saled* [*lo dikted ke lo ved veni* = he said he would come]. The suffix *-iv(i)* is to submit to the same rule as *-ione*; if the verb ends in *a*, *i*, or *o* a *-t-* is inserted between the full verb and the suffix [*afirm-a*, *afirm-a/t/iv; demonstr-a/t/iv, signifik-a/t/iv*]. As an alternative form for the suffix *-ere* the suffix *-tore* has been admitted with the same meaning: it is more international for certain words [*diktatore, kolaboratore*]; it may also be used for instruments [*akumulatore, elevatore, transformatore*]. The suffixes *-on* and *-ilo* are abandoned and *-mente* is used as the best substitute for *-ilo*. (*Novialiste*, 18, 1937.)

Novial differentiates between *kafe* = coffee and *kafee* = café. Jespersen now accepts that words ending in *-ee* should have the stress on the first *e*, an abrogation of the rule that the vowel preceding the last consonant should be stressed, with the exception of consonants used for flexion [*-s, -d, -m, -n*]. The new rules may also be formulated to say that the double *ee* is stressed as one long *e*. Two words have been changed back into the form in which they are found in Ido, *semper* into *sempre*, and *even* into *mem*, although *me-m* may also be the accusative of *me*.

c and *z*. In order to retain historic spelling in Novial against the original phonetic spelling which led to the suppression of both *c* and *z*, Jespersen has re-introduced both letters without distinctive pronunciation. He now distinguishes between phonetic Novial (F.N.) as hitherto used without *c* and *z*, and orthographic Novial (O.N.) admitting *c, ç, sc*, and *z*. An important rule is that *s, c, ç, sc, z* in O.N. are always to be pronounced as hard *s* [*sivil* or *civil, sientie* or *scientie, sone* or *zone*. *ç*, taken from F [*façade*], is pronounced as *s* before *a, o, u*, and is required if suffixes begin with the vowel *a, o*, or *u* [*nuançosi, françum, prinça*, but *nuance, Francia, prince*]. Similarly in the words *komença, komençant, komenço*.

In O.N. the *k*-sound before *a, o, u* and before consonants may be written with *c* [*cosmopoliti, succese*].

In O.N. Jespersen re-introduces the letter *y* as a vowel with the pronunciation of *i* [*sylabe, symbole, symetri, symfonie*].

In the *e/a/o* words Jespersen abandons the ending *-o* and uses the infinitive without any suffix. He says that linguists have known for a long time that the infinitive was originally a noun [*manca de dormi trubla me, ante li ariva del trene, vive es labora*].

The changes introduced are slight. To give a short example, a passage from Andersen's *The Emperor's New Clothes* is here reproduced in Orthographical Novial.

'Men Deo!' lo pensad, 'ob es posibli ke me es stupid? Tum me ha nulitem opinet, e tum nuli home darfa sava! Ob me non es habil por men oficie? No, vud es non-tolerabli ke me nara ke me non vida li texatu!'

'Nu, vu dicte nulum pri lu!' dicted un ek li texeres.

'O, lu es belisi! totim charmivi!' dicted li oldi ministro, regardant tra sen lunetes, 'dis desine e dis colores! Yes, me ve dicte al emperere ke lu plesa me tre multim!'

'Nu, tum plesira nus!' dicted li du texeres, e les nomad li kolores e li stranji desine. Li oldi ministro auscultad atentim, por tu pove dicte li samum, kand lo venid retro al emperere, e talim lo fad.'

(*Comparative Texts, International Auxiliary Language Association (IALA).*)

IV—7. Commentary

Novial has many features in common with Ido of which Jespersen was, to a large extent, a co-author during the years of the Delegation's activities. The most striking departure from the principles of Ido is his abolition of distinguishing vowel-endings to word-groups, the so-called pleonastic endings. It enabled Jespersen to devise the class of e/a/o words and similar groups, which represents a very noticeable solution to the problem of direct derivation. But the abolition of distinguishing vowel endings for word groups created a new set of problems which, according to many experienced interlinguists, makes the practical application of the language more difficult and also complicated the indirect derivation.

The adjectival ending -*i* is optional, but must be added if the adjective is used anaphorically with the plural -*s* [*li blank/is*]. It also is obligatory when used with the suffix -*osi* as otherwise it might stand for the plural form of -*o* [*kuraj/osi*]. It may be said, as Jespersen does, that the derivation in e/a/o does not clash with the noun forms ending in e/a/o indicating respectively neuter/feminine/masculine [*home, homa, homo*], but in practice it must mean a demand on memory to distinguish between the two uses of these endings.

The first exception which we shall consider is the group of a/o and e/o nouns derived from a verb. In both these cases the last vowel of the noun is replaced by -*o*, but if the verb ends in -*i* or -*u* we have to retain this final vowel [*defini/io*]. The second exception concerns the suffix -*ione*. If the verb ends in either a, i, or u it retains its ending and a -*t*- is inserted between the full verb and the ending. It is doubtful whether by saying that the -*t*- stands for the passive participle the rule becomes any easier. We have to add further that verbs ending in -*e* do not add the ending to the passive participle but suppress the ending -*e* and add the suffix to the root [*komunik/atione*, but *okas/ione*]. A similar exception applies to verbs to which the suffix -*eska* is added. Verbs ending in -*i* retain this vowel [*dorm-i/eska*] while verbs ending in either -*a* or -*e* suppress the final vowel and join the suffix to the root [*am/eska, kurs/eska*]. The final vowel in connexion with suffixes is generally suppressed if the suffix begins with a vowel, and retained if the suffix begins with a consonant.

-endi and *-indi* follow an exception [*lekt/indi*, but *expedi/indi*]. *-u* and *-i* remain, but *-a* and *-e* disappear before *-endi* or *-indi*. There is no possibility of formulating a rule which would apply to all cases and the learner will have to rely on his memory to use the derivatives correctly.

A further exception which should be mentioned here is the use of alternative affixes for the same meaning. Jespersen admits *-ere* and *-iste*, and in his subsequent changes also admitted *-tore* with a similar meaning. It is true that we can obtain derivatives which are more international through a variety of suffixes with the same or similar meaning. This is the naturalistic solution which leads away from precise expression and simplicity in word formation. The distinction made between *-um* and *-ure* seems rather subtle, and practice will have to show whether it is required. Jespersen himself pleaded for economy in language, saying rightly that a planned language cannot attempt to express all the shades of meaning in all ethnic languages.

Jespersen's Novial has many features which are advocated by the naturalistic school of interlinguists, the use of auxiliary verbs, the revised system of spelling, a certain number of flexional elements in indirect derivation, the abolition of so-called pleonastic endings, the plural form in *-s*. The introduction of the adverbial suffix *-ari* (*revolution/ari*) is superior to the Esperanto-Ido *-ema*. From Esperanto Jespersen has admitted, to some extent, the principle of sufficiency in indirect derivation.

On the whole Novial can be said to be midway between the extremes of naturalness and autonomy.

V. Interlingua (*Latino sine flexione*) (1903) by Giuseppe Peano

V—1. History

THE CHIEF AUTHOR OF Interlingua (abbreviated I.L. or L.s.f.) was Giuseppe Peano (1858—1932), professor of mathematics at the University of Turin. In 1908 Peano was elected President of the former *Kadem Bevünetik Volapüka*, a body which was later known as the *Akademi de Lingu Universal* and continued under Peano's leadership as the *Academia pro Interlingua*. In 1910 the *Academia* published its linguistic decisions in *Discussiones* ('Propositiones Approbato ab Academia'), and these decisions formed the grammatical basis of the system now known as *Interlingua* or *Latino sine flexione*. *Schola et Vita*, the official publication of the Academia pro Interlingua, was written in Interlingua but in order to encourage general research on problems of constructed auxiliary language it accepted contributions written in any other system. The International Auxiliary Language Association has included Interlingua in the list of systems of demonstrated usefulness.

Peano based his conception of an auxiliary language on the common word material of the European languages, and a revival of a simplified Latin, *i.e.*, a Latin without inflexions. His main contribution was the publication of his *Vocabulario Commune* which contained those roots which are common to the European languages. The 1915 edition contains 14,000 words which are in current use. Interlingua is considered to be the most extreme naturalistic system, containing a minimum of grammatical rules. Peano claims it to be immediately comprehensible to those with a knowledge of Latin. It accepts, with little or no modification, the existing scientific nomenclatures. In view of its universality Peano chose Latin spelling in preference to that of modern languages.

V—2. Grammar

The following three fundamental rules have been adopted by the Academy and show the very loose structure of the grammar of Interlingua: (1) Interlingua adopts every word common to English, German, French, Spanish, Italian, Portuguese, Russian and every

Anglo-Latin word; (2) Every word which exists in Latin has the form of the Latin stem, or root, or radical; (3) The suffix -s indicates the plural. (*Key to and Primer of Interlingua*, Kegan Paul, 1931.)

The *alphabet* comprises 9 vowels and the consonants as in English with some exceptions. The vowels are *a* [pr. as in *father*], *e* [*they, fate*], *i* [*machine*], *o* [*tone*], *u* [*rule*], *y* [pr. as French *u*], *j* [pr. as *y* in *yes*], *æ* [*aisle*], *œ* [*boil*]. The exceptions for consonants are *b* [pr. as English *b*, but like *p* if followed by *s* or *t*], *c* [always as *k*], *g* [pr. as *g* in *gold*], *h* [silent as in *th, ph, ch, rh*, otherwise like the English *h*], *q* [*qu* in quarrel], *r* [*correct*], *s* [*sound*], *t* [*time*], *v* [pr. as *w* or *v*], *x* [pr. as *ks*], *z* [*zeal*]. Interlingua admits alternative pronunciations for *y* and *j* [pr. as in *tin*], *æ* and *œ* [pr. as *a* in *fate* and *e* in *get* respectively], *b* [pr. always as English *b*], *h* [always silent], *ph* [pr. as *f*], *v* [pr. as English *v*]. Double consonants are used [*officiale*].

The *stress* falls on the penultimate syllable.

Article. There is no definite or indefinite article. The article is translated by a pronoun [*illo, uno*, etc.] when it has the value of a pronoun and when its use is necessary [*da ad me libro* = give me the book; *da ad me uno libro* = give me a book, etc.].

The singular *noun* has no specific grammatical ending. The Latin dictionary gives two forms for each noun, the nominative form and the genitive form [*rosa, rosæ; pes, pedis*]. The I.L. forms are taken from the genitive by changing *æ* into -*a; -i* into -*o; -us* into -*u; -ei* into -*e; -is* into -*e* [L *rosæ* = I.L. *rosa;* L *lauri* = I.L. *lauro; casus, casu; seriei, serie; pacis, pace*]. A few nouns are used in their nominative form [*mas* = male].

I.L. uses no one determinative ending for nouns in either singular or plural but derives its endings according to the three following rules based on Latin usage: (1) -*a* if the Latin nominative plural ends in -*a* [L *arma* = I.L. *arma* = arms]; (2) -*a* or -*as* if the plural nominative ends in -*æ* [L *divitiæ*, or *divitias* = riches]; (3) -*os* if the plural nominative ends in -*i* [L *liberi* = I.L. *liberos* = children]; -*e* or -*es* if the nominative plural ends in -*es* [L *majores* = I.L. *majore* or *majores* = ancestry].

The *plural* is expressed by -*s* added to the noun but is omitted where any other word indicates the plural [*patre habe filios et filias* = the father has sons and daughters, but *patre habe plure filio et plure filia*].

The *pronouns* are *me, te, illo* = he, she, it, him, her; *id* = it; *nos, vos, illos*. *Illa, illas* may be used as feminine forms. The reflexive pronoun is *se, se ipso* and may be used for oneself, himself, themselves.

The *possessive pronouns* are *meo, tuo, suo* (singular and plural), *nostro, vostro*. Alternative means of expressing the possessive forms are *de me, de te, de nos, de vos*.

The *verb in the infinitive* ends in -*re* [*ama/re*]. The present indicative is obtained by removing the infinitive ending [*me ama, te ama*].

The *past tense* is obtained without inflexion, and is either expressed by some other word indicating the past [*heri me scribe* = I wrote yesterday], or by an adverb as *jam, tum, in* or *e* preceding the verb [*me jam ama* = I loved, *me tum ama*, or *me e ama*].

The *future tense* is obtained without inflexion, and is either expressed by the addition of *in futuro*, or *vol* or *debe* as auxiliaries [*me vol ama* = I shall love, *me debe ama*] or by *i* preceding the verb [*me i ama*].

The *imperative form* is the same as the form for the present tense. The *optative* and *hortative* is the same as the *imperative, i.e.*, the form of the present tense.

The *passive voice* is formed with the verb *es* = to be and the past participle [*me es amato* = I am loved].

The *passive participle* is formed by adding *-to* to the present tense [*ama/to, filio es amato ab matre*]. The *active participle* is formed by adding *-nte* to the present tense [*ama/nte*].

The *adjective* is obtained from Latin by the following rules: (1) by leaving the nominative neuter of the Latin form unchanged when it ends in *-e* [L *celebre* = I.L. *celebre*], (2) by changing the nominative neuter of the Latin form to *-o* when it ends in *-um* [L *novum* = I.L. *novo*], (3) by changing the genitive form in all other cases from *-is* to *-e* [L *audacis* = I.L. *audace*].

The *adverbs* are obtained from adjectives by means of *cum mente, in modo* [*cum mente diligente* or *in modo diligente* = diligently; *in modo fraterne* = fraternally].

The *cardinal numbers* are: *uno, duo, tres, quatuor, quinque, sex, septem, octo, novem, decem; decem-uno* or *decem-et-uno*, etc.; *viginta* = 20, *triginta* = 30, *quadraginta* = 40, *quinquaginta* = 50, *sexaginta* = 60; *centum* = 100, *mille* = 1,000.

The *ordinal numbers* are: *primo, secundo, tertio, quarto, quinto, sexto, septimo, octavo, nono, decimo, decimo-primo*, etc.; *vigesimo* = 20th, *trigesimo* = 30th, *quadragesimo* = 40th, etc.; *centesimo* = 100th.

The *degrees of comparison* are expressed as follows : *breve* [short], *plus breve* or *magis breve* [shorter], *maximo breve* [shortest]; *breve, minus breve* [less short], *minimum breve* [least short].

Syntax: The word order is loose and not fixed by rigid rules, but generally follows the usage of English. The subject comes first, the verb last, but the latter may come first in the sentence if it is emphasized and if the sentence begins without introductory words. Adverbs usually follow the verb, but they precede the adjective if they modify it. Adjectives follow the noun which they modify.

There is no agreement between verb and subject in number and person. For that reason Interlingua is also called *Latino sine flexione*.

V—3. The affixes and their meaning

The affixes lack precise semantic values. They are taken from the ethnic languages and used in close analogy to their varying usages in these languages. In certain cases a suffix may require an additional

vowel between root and suffix but no definite rule is given to explain
the appearance of such vowel [-*atione* denotes ' a process' but in
Peano's list it appears as -*tione*].

This list contains only the most frequent prefixes and suffixes.

PREFIXES

anti-	[*anti/suffragista* = anti-suffragist]
auto-	[*auto/mobile, auto/inductione* = self-induction]
bene-	[*bene/dicto* = well said]
co-	[*co/operatore* = co-operator]
dis-	[*dis/membra* = dismember]
im-	[*im/mortale* = immortal]
in-	[*in/habilitate* = inability]
inter-	[*inter/acto* = interact]
male-	[*male/forma* = misform]
pan-	[*pan/asiatico* = pan-asiatic]
para-	[*para/producto* = by-product]
pseudo-	[*pseudo/nymo* = pseudonym]
quasi-	[*quasi/officiale* = quasi-official]
re-	[*re/examina* = re-examine]
sub-	[*sub/terraneo* = subterranean]
super-	[*super/homine* = superman]

Certain prepositions may be used as prefixes. *Mal(e)* may be used as a
prefix without its final *e*. The preposition *sine* = without, may stand for
the English suffix -*less*.

SUFFIXES

-*ismo*	[*protection/ismo* = protectionism]
-*ico*	[*electr/ico* = electric]
-*ido*	[*splend/ido* = splendid]
-*ista*	[*femin/ista* = feminist]
-*ale*	[*gener/ale* = general]
-*ano*	[*americ/ano* = American]
-*ario*	[*avi/ario* = aviary]
-*astro*	[*poet/astro* = poetaster]
-*bile*	[*sta/bile* = stable]
-*elo*, -*ela*	[*sequ/ela* = sequel]
-*ore*	[*col/ore* = colour]
-*tivo*	[*puni/tivo* = punitive]
-*oso*	[*fam/oso* = famous]
-*ato*	[*sublim/ato* = sublimate]
-*tore*	[*fac/tore* = maker]
-*tore*	[*ac/tore* = actor]
-*tate*	[*quali/tate* = quality]
-*tione*	[*declar/a/tione* = declaration]
-*tia*	[*tenden/tia* = tendency]
-*tia*	[*elegan/tia* = elegance]
-*io*	[*spectroscop/io* = spectroscope]
-*ia*	[*zoolog/ia* = zoology]
-*fica*	[*justi/fica* = justify]
-*esco*	[*statu/esco* = statuesque]

It will be difficult for the student to learn the affixes and their meaning
independently, and Peano suggests the frequent reading of Interlingua
literature for the acquisition of a correct and good style.

NUMERAL PARTICLES
singulo, uno per uno = one by one; *bino, trino, quatuor; simplice* = single, *duplo* = double; *dimidio* = one half, *un tertio* = a third; *semel, uno vice* = once, *bis, duo vice* = twice, *ter, tres vice* = three times, *quatuor vice* = four times.

V—4. Vocabulary
Peano claimed that Interlingua is a language with a minimum of grammatical rules, a claim illustrated by the following principle, 'the same word may be used as a verb or as a noun, either without any change or with a slight change of the ending in accordance with the rules. Adjectives may be used as adverbs.'

The vocabulary is almost exclusively Latin, but with the inflexions eliminated. A knowledge of Latin will be the best key to Interlingua as a few examples will show [*domina* = woman, Mrs; *gossypio* = cotton; *hebdomade* = week; *inquilino* = tenant of a house; *itinera* = to travel; *præsertim* = especially; *pyrsoscapho* = steamboat; *viatore* = traveller, passenger].

V—5. Comparative texts
(*The Emperor's New Clothes, by Hans Christian Andersen.*)

'O domino Deo!' illo cogita, 'possibile que me es stupido? Hoc me nunquam suppone, et hoc nullo debe sci! Possibile que me non es apto ad meo officio? Non, es re intolerabile si me dic que me non vide textura!'

'An, vos exprime nihil super id!' dic uno de textores.

'O isto es splendido! toto magnifico!' dic vetere ministro, dum examina per suo perspicillos, 'hoc designo et hoc colores! Certo, me vol dic ad imperatore que illo place ad me maximo modo!'

'Bene, hoc satisfac nos!' dic ambo textores, et illos mentiona nomines de colores et de extraordinario designo. Vetere ministro ausculta cum attentione, pro pote idem repete, quando illo redi ad imperatore, et ita illo fac. (*From the IALA Comparative Texts*).

(*A text written by the author, Giuseppe Peano, Discussiones*, II, 1, 1911)

Nostro Academia, in 1895, adopta principio de internationalitate maximo, et ex elementos commune ad linguas de Europa, in 1902, construe Neutral, lingua que conserva simplicitate de Volapük, et es intelligibile, sine studio aut quasi, ad omni homo culto de Europa. Plure alio auctore, ante et post Academia, perveni ad resultatu simile.

Ergo hodie existe novo scientia et arte, de scribe in modo intelligibile ad omni homo culto, que cognosce uno lingua de Europa. Vario manuale de interlingua, sub vario nomen, es vario tractatu de idem scientia.

Nominato, in 26. XII. 1908, directore de Academia, pro quinque anno, me applica ad nostro societate, que promove scientia de interlingua, methodo vigente in omni societate scientifico; id es, publicacione de 'Discussiones,' libero ad omni opinione, et ad omni experimento.

V—6. Commentary

If we compare Interlingua with Occidental we will discover a certain similarity of principle, the attempt of both languages at extreme naturalness. While Occidental has chosen as its base-languages the neo-Latin group, Interlingua has gone a step further back and taken Latin, but without inflexions. In fact it is *a posteriori* to such an extent that we can call it a modified and simplified form of Latin. To support this statement I quote from the *Key to Interlingua* (Academia pro Interlingua, 1927, Cavoretto) that 'if an Interlingua word is not immediately intelligible, any Latin school dictionary may be consulted to obtain the meaning.' Peano has attained what, in his view, is the main achievement of Interlingua, namely the absence of a rigid grammatical structure. He also mentions that a language with a minimum of grammar is easier to learn than one that has a great many rules. This is a simple statement of fact, but it does not follow that such a language is easier to handle. We have already seen that a previous knowledge, or partial knowledge, of Latin is highly desirable if we wish to express ourselves correctly in Interlingua. A language that is constructed with a minimum of grammatical rules cannot be as precise as one that has as its basis the simplified structure, but without exceptions, of the European languages.

The brief list of affixes contains two negative prefixes (*im-*, *in-*) which fulfil the same function and which are retained purely in analogy to the affixes in existing languages [E impossible, injustice]. To adopt, for a constructed language, two or more terms for the same function is a violation of the principle of economy. The suffix *-ore* in *col/ore* = colour is for all practical purposes a part of the root. It would be easier for the student to learn *colore* as a new word than to try to analyse it. The same applies to *sta/bile* and many other forms, and it will be very difficult to give a definition, satisfactory to the student and fair to the loose rules of the grammar of Interlingua, which will clearly describe the meaning of *-bile*, *-ela* [in *regu/ela*, *-tate* [in *quali/tate*], *-tia*, *-tore* [in *ac/tore*], *-esco* [in *statu/esco*], *-id* [in *splend/ido*] in all their possible connexions.

Interlingua has no exact rules of word derivation which would explain or, possibly, regulate a number of exceptions. So far as precise scientific expression and the use of modern technical terminology is concerned, Interlingua can have little importance, for with its present structure it cannot solve the requirements of a language that is claimed to be able to serve as an auxiliary language for all needs of modern culture and civilization. And it should be remembered that Interlingua has been designed for those who have a knowledge of Latin.

PART II

VI. A Priori and a Posteriori Principles

VI—1. Classification of language systems

LOUIS COUTURAT AND LEOPOLD LEAU classified the systems of constructed languages, as far as they were known to them, into three groups, (1) *a priori* systems, (2) mixed systems, and (3) *a posteriori* systems. Professor Guérard has given a good definition of these two terms in his short history, 'an *a priori* language is one which is based on some logical conception without any reference to existing forms; an *a posteriori* language is one that derives all its elements from natural tongues.'

The first *a priori* systems were called pasigraphies, *i.e.*, languages fit only for writing. The most important ones were quoted and reviewed by Couturat and Leau in their *Histoire*. They are mentioned to show that the beginnings of the thought of an artificial means of communication developed about 300 years ago. Descartes expressed his ideas on the subject in a letter to Mersenne in 1629, a thought which was taken up by Dalgarno in 1661, Wilkins in 1668, Leibniz in 1679, and Delormel in 1795. One of the first languages intended for speech was *Solresol* by Sudre (1817), which was based on the seven monosyllabic names of the gamut tones. From that time onward more and more systems were devised by various authors profiting by the experience of their predecessors. The most important of them were *Langue universelle et analytique* by Vidal (1844), the proposals by Renouvier to the *Société de Linguistique* (1855), *Lingualumina* by Dyer (1875), *Langue Internationale étymologique* by Reimann (1877), *Langue naturelle* by Maldant (1887), *Spokil* by Nicolas (1900), *Zahlensprache* by Hilbe (1901); and *Völkerverkehrssprache* by Dietrich (1902).

The mixed systems are those which take some elements from ethnic languages and add other elements and rules based on logical conceptions not found in any existing language. The best known system in this class was *Volapük* by Schleyer (1880). The name, *vola-pük*, is a deformation of *world speech*. *Volapük binom puk nen sesums*, means Volapük is a language without exceptions. It was archaic, difficult to learn, and not comprehensible without previous study. Other mixed systems were created at the same time but none of them survived the projects based, more or less, on the linguistic material of the ethnic languages, *Bopal* (1887), *Spelin* (1888), *Veltparl* (1896), *Langue bleue* (1899). The later systems have developed in the direction of greater ease of learning. A text in any modern system of constructed language can be understood at first sight by those who know several European languages while *a priori* or mixed systems retained the aspect of a code unintelligible to the outsider.

Of the *a posteriori* systems *Esperanto* had the most outstanding success. *Ido*, *Occidental*, *Novial*, and *Interlingua* have been briefly reviewed in previous chapters, being described as of demonstrated usefulness by IALA. *Interlingua* (*Latino sine flexione*) is a reformed system of Latin without inflexions but otherwise based on the vocabulary of Latin. Professor Yushmanov (University of Leningrad) collected data of over three hundred projects more or less fully developed, but only the five previously mentioned claim any following in different countries and a literature or magazines of their own. The experiences gained with these systems form the recognized basis for all future research for the planned language.

VI—2. An interpretation of the terms

Professor Collinson, in his commentary to the criteria of IALA, differentiates between extreme *a priorism* and modified *a priorism*, as well as between extreme *a posteriorism* and modified *a posteriorism*. Extreme *a priorism* has already been described as having no reference to existing forms. Modified *a priorism* is one in which the logical view-point prevails over the principle of conformity with ethnic languages. Extreme *a posteriorism* describes forms which are used with no or only slight modification of the forms of one or more ethnic languages. Collinson says that an extreme *a posteriori* language may be one which is entirely based on an ethnic language, reforming one part of it, for example English with a simplification of its spelling, or English with a restriction of its vocabulary, or Latin stripped of its inflexions and adding a number of auxiliary and international words.

Modified *a posteriorism* is a term applied by him to structural features of constructed languages which are adopted from ethnic languages to conform to certain rules and to the principles of a particular language. These modifications are examined in regard to roots, to word-building, and to grammatical structure. (1) The majority of roots are in international use and of Latin origin and a number of other roots have been added from other ethnic languages. (2) The affixes of ethnic languages which may have several functions are taken into the system and assigned one function only, *i.e.*, they become monosignificant (*Esperanto*, *Ido*). (3) Affixes may be taken from ethnic languages and their meaning may vary according to the usages in ethnic languages (*Occidental*). (4) The various grammatical patterns of the ethnic languages may be followed, and more or less rigidly adhered to.

The different existing systems of constructed language vary considerably in degree as to the principles of derivation, use of auxiliary verbs, meaning and selection of roots, and other word-building elements. We can say that the authors of the modern systems prefer on the whole *a posteriori* forms.

VII. Root Selection, Neologisms, and the Definition of Meaning

VII—1. The principle of root selection

THE GREATEST POSSIBLE INTERNATIONALITY of the roots should be one of the guiding principles for the selection of the vocabulary of the planned language. How can we obtain this maximum internationality? We know that each great ethnic language is spoken by a definite number of people. A root which is common to the greatest number of European languages, which form the basis of our language, is a root which can be accepted. It only remains to find the common form of that root, as it may vary in different languages. Each language possesses a number of technical words often of foreign origin. English words in daily use may be known by a synonymous root which may be an international or foreign word, and this foreign word may in turn be understood in several other ethnic languages, *e.g.*, 100 is in English *hundred*, in German *hundert*, in Danish *hundrede*, yet the root *cent* has long been familiar through *per cent*. (D *Prozent*), *centimetre*, *centennial*, *century*, *centenary*, D *Zentner*, Danish *centner*. A third group is found in those words which are of the same origin but differ slightly from language to language. These differences have grown through phonetic development. As the planned language must possess a common pronunciation, we select a combination of letters which conform to the rules of pronunciation without losing the visual familiarity of the word form. *Change* is the same in English and French, but to preserve the known pronunciation according to the rules of the planned language we adopt *chanj-* (or *ŝanĝ-* if we select Esperanto). The Romanic form will often be decisive as it conforms with one of the forms in French, Spanish, or Italian, and often with Latin. Thus the planned language will be rather more Romanic than Germanic.

The languages generally referred to as DEFIRS (German-English-French-Italian-Russian-Spanish) were generally the basis of root-selection but if no common root could be found the Latin vocabulary was consulted. A few examples may illustrate the method applied for the selection of the roots of Ido:

D	Wind	gross	Acker (Agronom)	Geld (pekuniar)
E	wind	grand (big)	acre (agriculture)	money (pecuniary)
F	vent	grand	champ (agriculture)	argent (pécuniaire)
I	vento	grande	agro	denaro (pecuniario)
S	viento	grande	campo	dinero (pecuniario)
Ido	*vent/o*	*grand/a*	*agr/o*	*pekuni/o*

There was very little difficulty in choosing the words *vento* and *granda*, in the first two cases. In the third and fourth examples the ethnic words differ so widely that it was necessary to take into consideration any words of foreign origin which might provide a common root. Other problems arose which it was more difficult to solve. *Arm* has two distinct meanings. The meaning 'arm' (limb) agrees in English, German, and the Scandinavian languages, but in the sense of weapon it agrees in EFSI, and is known through foreign words *armée* in DEFR, I *armata*, S *armada*, etc. We have to retain *arm/* for the meaning of weapon and choose a Romanic form for the meaning of limb, *braki/* as found in em*brace*. In certain cases arbitrary changes become unavoidable as in *pord/o* = door instead of *port/o*, for we have to retain the latter root for *port/ar* = to carry. Jespersen quotes a very fine example of conflicting terms for the idea of *soul* (*International Language and Science*, 1910). The English root 'soul' cannot be accepted as the diphthong *ou* could not be rendered. We cannot take over the word in the form of *sol* because it is required for the meaning 'alone' (IS *solo*, internationally used in music, E *sole*, F *seul*) and we cannot take it over as *sul* as this is required for the meaning of 'soil'. D *Seele* is not familiar enough to a sufficient number of people, and *sel* is further required for the meaning of 'saddle' (FIS). The French word *âme* is not sufficiently widely known and the root *am* is required for the meaning of 'love' (FIS and derivatives in E). The use of the Latin *anim-*, which is the basis of the Romanic languages, is excluded, as we must consider it in relation to possible affixes. Connected with the suffix *-al* = related to, it would result in *animal* which would then mean partly 'relating to the soul' and partly 'animal', which is impossible. To avoid these complications we must slightly alter the root itself and we get *anm/o*. The task of obtaining the most international form which causes no misunderstanding is not always easy. The 10,000 odd roots in Ido have been selected according to the principles enumerated above. Couturat has supplied some valuable statistics which show the internationality of the vocabulary. He counted the roots contained in the first dictionaries (5,379) and found that the following numbers occurred in the ethnic languages:

French 4,880, or 91 per cent.
Italian 4,454, „ 83 „ „
Spanish 4,237, „ 79 „ „
English 4,219, „ 79 „ „
German 3,302, „ 61 „ „
Russian 2,821, „ 52 „ „

L. H. Dyer based his table on the same dictionaries (*The Problem,* 1923):

2,024 roots, or 38 per cent., belong to 6 languages						
942	,,	,, 17	,,	,,	5	,,
1,111	,,	,, 21	,,	,,	4	,,
585	,,	,, 11	,,	,,	3	,,
454	,,	,, 8	,,	,,	2	,,
255	,,	,, 5	,,	,,	1	language

The number of affixes enlarges the range of these roots.

VII—2. The vocabulary of Esperanto and the use of neologisms

The original *Universala Vortaro* contained 2,629 roots (Stojan's count). The six *Aldonoj* contained nearly 2,000 roots and another 1,400 to 1,500 have come into common use according to rule 15 of Zamenhof's grammar. These words are mainly of a scientific character and equivalent terms may already exist in Esperanto constructed from the original word building material [*mal/san/ul/ej/o* = a place for people who are the opposite of healthy, or the newer term *hospitalo*]. Particularly in scientific works new terms will be used which have not yet found their way into the Esperanto vocabulary, but they have to be used because adequate translation of these notions would be impossible without the use of such terms. These neologisms are introduced by various authors and it is theoretically possible that in a general application of Esperanto, simultaneously in many countries, different authors may define and spell such terms in varying ways which would give rise to confusion. It would be preferable if some sort of linguistic authority would sanction a definite form and a definition of the meaning of such scientific terms, which should be accepted by writers in all countries.

The roots selected by Zamenhof are more artificial than those of Ido [Esp. *raci/o,* Ido *racion/o,* adj. *raci/a, racion/al/a;* Esp. *antaŭen-puŝi,* Ido *propulsar,* etc.]. The *Esperanto-Ido Dictionary* (London 1934) contains over 2,000 roots which differ. For some terms Esperanto uses composite words where Ido has adopted new roots. In compiling this dictionary I found that for a number of Ido roots there existed no possible Esperanto equivalent.

Jespersen mentions that some peculiarities of the Esperanto vocabulary may be accounted for by the Slavonic mother-tongue of the author. His preference for sibilants and diphthongs is especially evident in the invented words [*ĉi, ĉiu, eĉ, ĝi, ĝis*]. He quotes a phrase from Zamenhof's *Krestomatio* (p. 288): . . *ĉiuj tiuj senantaŭjuĝaj kaj honestaj homoj, kiuj, anstataŭ filizofadi pri ĝi* . . which would read in Ido: . . . *omna ica neprejudikoza e honesta homi, qui vice filozofiar pri ol* . . .

Esperanto has a greater number of Germanic roots than other systems and one reason advanced in favour of these roots is that they are shorter and consequently more convenient. A brief comparative table, below, will prove this point. It will have to be decided whether brevity is preferable to forms which are more international and which, in consequence, offer greater ease of learning to the greater number.

VII—3. *A comparison of Germanic and Romanic roots*

The subsequent selections from the comparative study by Professor Collinson gives an indication of the importance of Germanic roots in the various systems of planned languages. Where Esperanto, Ido, and Novial agree (*varm/* = warm) Occidental has chosen a Latin root (*calid*). The examples quoted here are simply given as translations, irrespective of their Germanic or Romanic origin.

The English or German terms enclosed in brackets differ phonetically from the root adopted in one or all of the systems.

English/German	Esperanto	Ido	Novial	Occidental
(coloured, motley)/bunt	diverskolora (bunta)	bunta	bunt(i)	multicolori
cheap/(billig)	malkara (malkosta)	chipa	chip(i)	modic
cold/kalt	malvarma	kolda	kold(i)	frigid
(wire)/Draht	drato	metalfilo	drate	stalfil
fish/Fisch	fiŝo	fisho	fishe	pisc
frost/Frost	frosto	frosto	froste	frigore
hair/Haar	haro	haro	hare	capille
(bright)/hell	hela	klara	klar(i)	clar
kernel/Kern	kerno	kerno	kerne	nucleo
kiss/küssen	kisi	kisar	basia	besar
loud/laut	laŭta	lauta	laut(i)	vocos
malt/Malz	malto	malto	malte	malt
milk/melken	melki	melkar	milka	melcar
month/Monat	monato	monato	mensu	mensu
often/oft	ofte	ofte	ofte	sovente
old/alt	maljuna	olda	old(i)	veli
stool (chair)/Stuhl	seĝo (skabelo)	stulo	stule	stul
(hit)/treffen	trafi	atingar	atena	tirar precis
(bird)/Vogel	birdo	ucelo	fogle	avio
ware/Ware	varo	varo	vare	merce
warm/warm	varma	varma	varm(i)	calid

In cases where all four languages disagree [*birdo, ucelo, fogle, avio; trafi, atingar, atena, tirar precis*] we may say that no system has found a completely satisfactory solution. In other cases Esperanto, Ido, and Novial agree, while Occidental has chosen a different root, often from Latin [*varma, varma, varm(i), calid; haro, haro, hare, capille; frosto, frosto, froste, frigore; varo, varo, vare, merce*, etc.]. In some cases all four systems agree, and we may assume that this choice would be final for the planned language [*malto, malto, malte, malt; melki, melkar, milka, melcar*]. Where Esperanto uses the prefix *mal-* [*malkara, malvarma, maljuna*, etc.] it would add to the internationality of the planned language to introduce the root already known [*chip, kold, old*].

VII—4. *The meaning of roots*

Jespersen defines the root as 'what is common to a certain number of words felt by the popular instinct of the speakers as etymologically belonging together' (*Language*, XIX, 6). We can discover common roots in derivatives which, according to their meaning have no apparent connexions. Jespersen quotes *roul-* in *rouler, roulement roulage, roulier, rouleau, roulette, roulis*. To establish a common root is only justifiable, according to him, if we do not think that this root gives us the ultimate explanation of these words. R. Berger (*Cosmoglotta*, XV, 4) has given some common roots as they appear in Occidental. He tries to prove a certain regularity in root selection:

gress	*firm*	*genera*
a/gress/er	a/firm/ar	genera/r
a/gress/ion	a/firm/ation	genera/tor
a/gress/or	a/firm/ativ	genera/tion
a/gress/iv	con/firm/ar	genera/tiv
a/gress/iv/ità	con/firm/ation	
pro/gress	in/firm	
pro/gress/er	in/firm/ità	
pro/gress/ion	in/firm/eria	
pro/gress/ist		
pro/gress/iv		
re/gress/ion		
re/gress/iv		
trans/gress/er		
trans/gress/ion		
di/gress/er		
di/gress/ion		
con/gress		
con/gress/ist		

The meaning in common between *generation* and *generator* is practically non-existent in everyday speech. The average person would not think to derive *agression* and *congress* from the same original root. In fact, R. Berger would find it difficult to give an acceptable definition of the roots *gress, firm, genera* which could be maintained for all derivatives.

For the purposes of the planned language the historic origin of the word is of little significance. What matters is the meaning of the root and the possibility of forming derivatives which retain the basic meaning. In Jespersen's opinion the meaning of the root in ethnic languages is somewhat vague and indeterminate. The planned language should be able to give definitions to its roots which are monosignificant and which can maintain this basic meaning through all their derivatives.

VII—5. *On analogical formations*

In speech, analogical formations are used preferably for forms which are the result of the correct application of the rules of each

language, according to Herman Paul. When the Indo-European
languages divided themselves into different language families, roots,
stems, and affixes did not exist, but only complete words. It is only
this material which furnishes the words which we use in our daily
speech. We no longer use autonomically the elements, roots, and
affixes, to make up the words required. The separate elements did
not continue their life in isolation. They gradually grew, according
to the laws of association, in groups which corresponded to grammatical categories, but they were never quite clear to the speaker
without previous instruction and thought. In the beginning, according to Paul, these groups were an aid to memory and helped the
growth of new combinations. That is what he describes as an analogical formation.

Each one of us, in speech, constantly creates analogical forms.
Reproduction from memory, or a new formation in analogy to
similar forms known, may be equally strong factors. If a person uses
'Milben' it may be that he learned this form from somebody else, or
that he may have heard the singular 'Milbe' and knowing that the
plural of 'Schwalbe' is 'Schwalben,' or the plural for 'Lerche' is
'Lerchen', he may unconsciously associate 'Milbe-Milben'. Or it
may be that he already knows the plural form 'Milben', but that it
might not have impressed him deeply enough at the time without an
association with similar ideas which now help him to memorize this
form. It is often impossible to discern clearly the part that memory
or creative fantasy might have played.

Analogical formations in ethnic languages may lead to forms which
are grammatically incorrect, a frequent occurrence in German:
tragen, trug; schlagen, schlug; fragen, 'frug' instead of the correct
form *'fragte'*.

For the planned language the problem does not arise if we agree
that each affix shall have only one function and one meaning. Any
analogical form so created with the same affix applied to a new verb
just learned will be grammatically quite correct. If we further remember that an auxiliary language will be taught in schools with
some grammatical explanation of the meaning of these elements at a
time when the student, however young, will already possess a basic
mastery of his own tongue, the danger of wrong analogies can be
averted. The risk of incorrect forms could only remain if the affixes
used in our planned language were selected from the ethnic languages with their varying usages and were not monosignificant, a solution advocated by the naturalistic school.

VII—6. *Selection of roots from the Indo-European languages*

IALA has expressed its preference for the selection of roots from
Indo-European languages. It justifies this preference on the
grounds of the dissemination of the Indo-European languages. The
following European countries have an I.-E. language as their chief

official language: Great Britain, Ireland, France, Germany, Italy, Russia, Spain, Portugal, Greece, Holland, Belgium, Iceland, Denmark, Norway, Sweden, Lithuania, Latvia, Poland, Czecho-Slovakia, Yugo-Slavia, Bulgaria, and Albania. In European countries where a non-I.-E. is the official language, some other I.-E. language is widely known: Estonia (German), Finland (Swedish), Hungary (German), Basque provinces (Spanish), Turkey (French, German). The I.-E. family is represented in Asia by Armenian, Persian, and some important Indian languages as Hindi, Bengali, Marathi, Gujarati. In North and South America we find English, French, Spanish, and Portuguese, in Australia English, and in Africa several European languages through cultural influences and colonization.

The I.-E. languages have a close resemblance to each other in structure. Peoples of I.-E. languages show great similarity in their way of thinking, if compared with thought-expression of Asiatic or African races. This offers much common ground for the building of the planned language which could not be found if it were to be based on the languages of the whole world. To obtain an easy and universal language, in the latter case, would be an impossibility.

A question of principle which IALA has carefully studied is that of univocity or monosignificance. The autonomists agree that this is a principle much to be desired, but they realize that no ethnic or constucted language could completely satisfy this principle without increasing its vocabulary to the extent of imparcticability. It is a principle which is, and can only be, followed to the fullest extent practicable.

Even in a constructed language the problem of metaphors still arises, and descriptive terms for machinery, etc. (the leg of a machine the screw head, etc.) might still have to be admitted. Couturat has suggested that metaphors should be avoided where clearer expression is possible, and should only be admitted in cases which can be assumed to be generally understood. If this principle is followed, metaphors should not give rise to serious misunderstandings.

VIII. Direct and Indirect Derivation

(The term *derivation* indicates the relation of words in various groups, *i.e.*, verbs, nouns, adjectives, adverbs. It is not used to indicate the etymological origin of a word.)

INTERLINGUISTS GENERALLY AGREE THAT the problem of derivation is one of the most important for the future planned language. The principles and rules of the present systems differ so widely that it has so far been impossible to formulate a final solution. We cannot model these rules exclusively on the ethnic languages because they are not regular, and we cannot contrive some purely *a priori* solution which would prove too difficult in everyday use. The only thing we can do is to compare the fundamental principles of each system to get a clear idea of the problem itself and its possible solutions.

In chapters I-IV the rules governing derivation in each of the four systems have been summarized. A comparative examination of these proposals can now be attempted which will more fully illustrate the problems involved.

VIII—1. Derivation in ethnic languages

The ethnic languages use both indirect (or mediate, *i.e.*, by means of a medium), and direct (or immediate) derivation. In indirect derivation affixes are used to modify the root [*change, unchangeable, changeability; resist, resistible, irresistible, resistibility*, etc.]. The method of indirect derivation is exact if the meaning of the affix in use is monosignificant, *i.e.*, if it stands for one meaning only and is invariable. We do not learn our mother tongue by an analysis of these elements but rather by the use of ready-made forms, and later by analogy to forms so learnt. Learning is made more difficult for the foreigner when he discovers a number of affixes which apparently fulfil the same or very similar functions [*ir*-resistible, *il*-logical, *un*-natural, *in*-variable, *de*-centralize, *dis*-interested, *mis*-represent, etc.].

Far more difficult to master are the usages of direct derivation which have been shaped by convention, and which vary considerably from one language to another. A nominal or substantival root is used to derive the verb directly, *i.e.*, without the addition of an affix or a new verbal root. Examples in English are very common, and the meaning of the verb thus derived is fixed solely by usage. *Shop, to shop*, meaning to visit a shop with intent to purchase, *ship, to ship*, meaning to transport goods by means of ships, *paper, to paper*, meaning to affix paper to something, for example to paper a room;

99

iron, to iron, meaning to smooth linen, etc., with iron, or to shackle with iron according to the context used; *chain, to chain*, meaning to secure or confine with chains; *house, to house*, meaning to provide one or several people with habitation, the housing problem; *to table* a bill in the House, but German (*auf-*)*tafeln*, or *-tischen* means to dish up food, to present food; *to feather* one's nest, *to book* a seat, *to water* a plant, etc. This practice extends equally to adjectives from verbs or vice versa [*dry, dry; cool, cool; warm, warm; clean, clean; open, open*], and adjectives from nouns [*secret, secret; equal, equal; right, right*]. We may assume that these usages are familiar to all who have an adequate knowledge of English, and for them direct derivation is a very convenient way of expression. The difficulty only arises when this kind of convention is carried into the making of a planned language which should be equally easy for all who use it. For the meaning attached to verbs derived from nominal roots varies in the ethnic languages. Professor Stör (University of Prague) has given some examples which illustrate these divergencies. In German *Feder* is used as a verb *federn* with three meanings, (1) to tar and feather, (2) to adorn with feathers, (3) to be elastic, *Feder* being the translation of *feather* and *spring*. In French *plume* becomes *plumer* with a completely different conventional meaning, it does not mean to adorn with feathers, but to pluck feathers. The meaning of *to chain* happens to agree in English and German, but in French *chaîner* means to measure with a chain [*mesurer avec la chaîne*]. We can well imagine that an auxiliary language which permits the direct derivation of nominal roots may cause considerable misunderstandings among those people who use this rule according to the traditions of their own language. The science of interlinguistics is today sufficiently advanced to enable us to avoid such complications in the planned language.

Another classification may here be of interest; it has already been used to examine some systems of planned language in previous chapters. It was proposed by Schleicher under the influence of Hegel. Two elements were distinguished by him, the elements carrying meaning, roots or full words, and the other elements which serve to indicate grammatical relations, affixes and terminations. Firth (*The Tongues of Men*) gives three formulae to illustrate the type of language:

(1) Meanings indicated by words, relations by position. R = root or full word, a = affix (prefix and suffix).

$$R^1 + R^2 + R^3 + R^4.$$

(*I wish (to) go there.*) These were called the Isolating or Positional languages.

(2) Meanings carried by invariable root, relations by affixes which may be monosignificant.

$$a + R + a + a$$

(*un-desir-ab-ility*).

These were called agglutinative languages.

(3) Meaning-roots and relational elements which became fused and formed an entity with a new meaning.

$p + R + s^{123}$ = (prefix plus root which may be modified [*drink, drank, drunk*] plus suffix or suffixes. The suffix or suffixes necessitate an inflexion of the final root-letter or letters [*concede, conce/ss/ion*]). These are called flexional languages.

The languages quoted by Firth for the first pattern were Chinese and English, for the second Turkish, Swahili, Tamil and Korean, for the third Sanskrit, Arabic, Greek, and Latin.

If this classification is applied to systems of planned languages the first pattern would describe some *a priori* projects, the second Esperanto and Ido, and the third—to some extent—Occidental.

We have to qualify this statement in classifying a particular language according to one of the three patterns, knowing that certain characteristics of other patterns may be found in its structure. In saying that Occidental is flexional, we must also acknowledge that many words are formed according to the agglutinative pattern, but the admission of flexional elements in contrast to the other systems makes this an outstanding characteristic.

Again for the flexional pattern we shall distinguish the so-called internal and external flexion. One example, taken from English solely to illustrate the term internal flexion [*sing, sang, sung*], is not used in any stem of planned language.

The term 'external flexion' as used in this book describes the change of the last letter of the root itself, *e.g.*, comprehen*d* and comprehen*s*ibility, in which the *d* has been changed into *s*. Occidental uses external flexion for a number of words and for some exceptional cases, as we have seen in Chapter III.

In applying Schleicher's classification to the present systems of planned languages, Occidental, containing a number of flexional characteristics, would rank as the highest developed system. Jespersen, however, outlines a different theory (*Language*, XXI, 7, 8). He finds that in early languages the number of irregularities, exceptions, anomalies, is greater than in modern ones. 'It is true that we not infrequently see new irregularities spring up where the formations were formerly regular, but these instances are very far from counter-balancing the opposite class, in which words once irregularly inflected become regular, or are given up in favour of regularly inflected words. The tendency is more and more to denote the same thing by the same means in every case, to extend the meaning, or whatever it is, that is used in a large class of words to express a certain modification of the central idea, until it is used in all other words as well.' Jespersen thus traces the simpler forms as the result of development from more archaic formations. He does not propose to reverse the theory 'isolating-agglutinative-flexional' into 'flexional-agglutinative-isolating.' Jespersen's opinion on the development of language after an enquiry of some 400 pages based on a life-long study is briefly and clearly stated, 'the evolution of language shows a progressive tendency from inseparable irregular conglomerations to freely and regularly combinable short elements.' If this dictum is acceptable to linguists who will formulate the coming form of a planned language, the system is likely to be based on the structural features of a perfected Esperanto-Ido type.

VIII—2. Derivation in planned systems

Direct derivation is said to offer greater facility in the use of a planned language but surrenders for it some precision of expression. In the following paragraph we shall examine the rules of the four main systems in employing, more or less, direct and indirect derivation.

The examples in direct derivation of nominal roots given in the previous paragraph show that ethnic languages do not always agree on the meaning of the verbs thus derived. There are, however, examples where the meaning coincides in all languages and they have formed the basis of a long discussion in interlinguistic circles which has never yet been finally settled. A few typical examples may illustrate this point :

English	French	German
crown, to crown	couronne, couronner	Krone, krönen
hammer, to hammer	marteau, marteler	Hammer, hämmern
pepper, to pepper	poivre, poivrer	Pfeffer, pfeffern
oil, to oil	huile, huiler	Oel, oelen

Esperanto

As we have seen in Chapter I Esperanto uses direct derivation which is not limited by any definite rule. The user of Esperanto may apply these forms throughout or limit himself to cases which are also to be found in ethnic languages and on which agreement of choice exists, as in the above examples. The verbs *kroni, marteli, pipri, olei,* which are understood by people knowing one of the great European languages, are directly derived from their respective nouns.

Some Esperantists have used the forms *jes-i* and *ne-i* meaning respectively 'to say yes' and 'to say no', or 'to affirm' or 'answer affirmatively', and 'to negate' or 'to deny'. Some such forms are ambiguous even to the experienced Esperantist and it would be better to replace them with new verbal roots. The necessity to use these forms in Esperanto is explained by the lack of adequate word-material. The *English-Esperanto (Edinburgh)* dictionary gives affirm = *certigi,* besides *firmdiri, jesi;* literally, however, *cert-igi* means to make certain. In this case, as in many others, the necessity for an ampler vocabulary must be faced if precision is to be attained. *afirmi* would well fit into the Esperanto vocabulary in the same way as it exists in the vocabulary of Ido.

The suffix *-ad-* in Esperanto stands for 'duration' or 'continuation' of an action but is widely used to distinguish the verbal noun from the nominal root from which the verb, in turn, was derived. We thus have the original word *kron-o* = the crown, *kron-i* = to crown, *kron-ad-o* = the act of crowning, coronation. Esperanto goes even further than ordinary direct derivation. It admits certain word building elements as complete words. The suffix *estr-* may become a complete noun by adding the grammatical termination *-o* to it, and thus stand for *master*. This practice is quite common and gives an air of artificiality to the language which could be avoided by using the known roots of the European languages.

A very important feature of Esperanto is the acceptance of the rule of 'necessity and sufficiency' proposed by R. de Saussure and accepted by the *Lingva Komitato*, *i.e.*, 'The formation of any constructed word is obtained by combining all the word elements (roots, affixes, and terminations) which are necessary and sufficient to evoke clearly the idea to be represented.' To appreciate the importance of this decision we shall have to examine more fully the practices of *indirect* (or *mediate*) *derivation* in Esperanto.

Zamenhof has formulated the rule that, given the root, the noun is formed by adding *-o* to it, the adjective by adding *-a*, the adverb by adding *-e*, the infinitive by adding *-i*, etc. It follows that grammatical terminations are interchangeable, but there exists no rule to define the exact meaning of the words thus obtained. It is important that all forms should carry a definite meaning. The practice to add grammatical terminations to elements without a clarification of meaning is—as we have seen in Esperanto—extended not only to roots but also to affixes which are treated as roots.

Lébasnier distinguishes three cases, (1) that of a derivative which may have several meanings. The relation between verb and noun may, as in ethnic languages, vary considerably in meaning [*brosi* = to act by means of a brush; *versi* = to make verses; *ori* = to cover with a coat of gold; *violoni* = to play on a violin]. Adjectives directly derived from nouns may also express different relationships [*orfa* = who *is* an orphan; *herba* = that which *contains* herbs; *sulfuro* and *sulfura*, but *fero* and *feraĵo*]; (2) that of one affix which may express different ideas. The suffix *-ad-* indicates 'repetition' of *paf/o* in *paf/ad/o*, 'the act of providing with a crown in *kron/o, kron/ad/o*. The suffix *-ul-* = characterized by, is used in *virg/ul/o* but considered superfluous in *vidvo*, used in *skeptikulo* but not in *katoliko*, in *mistikulo* but not in *elektito*; (3) that of a similar idea which may be expressed by different affixes. The suffixes *-il-* and *-aĵ-* are frequently interchangeable [*baraĵo, barilo*], and again justified by the rule of de Saussure we find *sano* and *saneco*, *abomena* and *abomeninda, fiksi* and *fiksigi*. The failure of Esperanto to apply a more precise and scientific derivation has often been put forward as a serious criticism and will be familiar to those who have occupied themselves with the problem of an auxiliary language for many years. Although it is an old argument, it will have to be considered as Esperanto is one of the systems which may be selected as a base project for the coming planned auxiliary language.

Most roots in Esperanto belong to a certain grammatical category. It may be verbal, nominal, or adjectival, according to whether the first derivative is a verb, a noun, or an adjective. Consequently we must know the root-word of each word-family in order to know to which grammatical category it belongs. We then form all other derivatives according to the rules which apply to each category. Such classification is arbitrary and leads to contradictions. We find *friponi* (verb) and *fripono* (noun), besides *hipokriti* and *hipokritulo*. The explanation is that *fripon-* is a nominal root from which we may directly derive the verb *friponi; hipokrit-* is a verbal root, and 'the person who is characterized by . . .' should be derived by means of the suffix *-ul-*, which gives us *hipokritulo*.

This derivation leads to further complications. From *armi* = to arm Esperanto derives *armilo* = weapon, but literally it would mean *instrument with which to arm; sen/arm/ig/i* according to the dictionary means to disarm. If *arm-* is a verbal root and means *to arm*, then the opposite should be *mal-armi; sen/arm/ig/i* = to render without arms is only correct if we accept *arm-* as a nominal root, which is not the case in Esperanto.

Ido

The rules of Ido do not admit of direct derivation of verbs from nominal roots as these roots do not express either an action or a state. To express the meanings to crown, to hammer, to pepper, to oil, Ido uses a number of precise and invariable affixes, *kron/iz/ar* = to equip or supply with a crown, *martel/ag/ar* = to act with a hammer, *pepr/iz/ar, ole/iz/ar*. For Ido the rule of reversibility has become part of its grammar. 'Every derivative must be reversible; that is to say, if one passes from one word to another of the same family in virtue of a certain rule, one must be able to pass inversely from the second to the first in virtue of a rule which is exactly the inverse of the preceding' (Courturat). In Ido we distinguish between verbal root and nominal root, the former expressing an action or a state [*labor-, drink-, parol-*] while the latter denotes an object (living being or thing), or expresses an aspect of it (as adjectives). Verbal roots produce the verb by adding the appropriate grammatical ending [*labor/ar, drink/ar, parol/ar*] and a noun directly derived from them can only mean the action, 'working', 'drinking', 'speaking'. Nominal roots can produce, by direct derivation, only names of beings or things or descriptions: 'man', 'house', 'beautiful', 'blind,' [Ido *homo, domo, bela, blinda*]. If we depart from a verbal root and wish to derive the noun [*labor/ar, labor/o* = to work, the work] we do not, in Ido, require an affix, as the verbal noun so derived does not contain any idea which is not already expressed by the verb. It follows that Ido cannot admit the direct derivation of verbs from nouns which do not express an action or a state.

The derivation in Ido is direct when it consists in changing grammatical terminations; infinitive in *-ar*, noun singular in *-o*, adjective in -*a*, adverb in -*e*. The verbal root *parol*- may be changed into *parolar*=to speak, *parolo*=speaking, *parola*=oral, *parole*=orally.

The derivation is indirect when it requires affixes. These affixes, as well as the roots, are invariable and modify but do not change the meaning. Affixes are not used in simple imitation of the ethnic languages [*varm/a* = warm, *varm/et/a* = lukewarm (little warm), *varm/eg/a* = hot].

For the direct (immediate) derivation Ido observes three rules which regulate the relationship between verbal, nominal, and adjectival roots. (1) The noun immediately derived from the verb signifies the state or action expressed by the verb [*labor/ar* = to work, *labor/o* =the work]. (2) The adjective directly derived from a noun describes how the thing or being is [*orfan/o* = orphan, *orfan/a infanto* = orphan child; *arjento* = silver, *arjenta kuliero* = silver spoon]. Inversely we may derive a noun from an adjective with the meaning 'the thing or being which is' [*richa* = rich, *richo* = a rich person; *blinda* = blind, *blindo* = a blind person; *dezerta* = deserted, *dezerto* = a desert]. (3) An adverb directly derived from an adjective expresses 'of the manner' indicated by the adjective [*bela* = beautiful, *bele* = beautifully; *agreabla* = agreeable, pleasant, *agreable* = agreeably, pleasantly]. The adverb directly derived from a noun forms the complement expressing the circumstances of place, time, quantity or quality [*automobile vehar* = to ride by car; *necese ajornar* = to adjourn of necessity; *telefone parolar* = to talk by telephone].

We cannot, in Ido, derive directly a verb from the adjective or a verb from a noun as there is no relationship which could be logically fixed. They would contradict the rule of reversibility (see Chapter II).

Occidental

Occidental does not use direct derivation as freely as Esperanto. The derivation of verbs from nominal roots is restricted to four cases, namely, when the meaning of the verb so derived indicates (1) to provide with, (2) to use as an instrument, (3) to secrete, and (4) to act as. Any cases which conform to these four categories may be directly derived. Thus Occidental forms *coron, coronar, pipre, piprar, martel, martelar*. S. Auerbach (*Pri nonmediati derivatione in li international lingues*) observes that, as the infinitive ending is -*r* only, no explanation is given for the addition of -*a*- in these cases. The verbal noun is formed by the affix -*ation, coron/ation, martel/ation*.

In Chapter III we have already seen the departure of Occidental from lines to which former systems have, more or less, conformed. The affixes used do, in some cases, cover a variety of meanings and examples given need not be repeated here. The model for their use could be found in most cases in the Romanic languages. Occidental does not attempt to introduce a simple and regulated system of derivation. The result was a far more natural aspect of the language and greater flexibility at the cost of precision of meaning of the derivatives so obtained.

Novial

Novial does not use the vowels -*o*, -*a*, -*e*, as do Esperanto and Ido, to indicate respectively the noun in singular, the adjective and the adverb. These three vowels in Novial have two distinct functions (1) to indicate the sexes [-*o* masculine, -*a* feminine, -*e* neuter] and (2) -*e* the noun or name, -*a* the verbal infinitive, -*o* the verbal noun expressing the action or state.

Direct derivation with these distinctive grammatical terminations, is used for the following three cases, (1) to use an instrument [*hamre* = the hammer, *tu hamra* = to hammer, *hamro* = hammering, *telefone* = the telephone, *tu telefona* = to telephone, *telefono* = telephoning; *bicikle* = the bicycle, *tu bicikla* = to cycle, *biciklo* = cycling], (2) to secrete [*sange* = the blood, *tu sanga* = to bleed, *sango* = bleeding; *sudore* = the sweat, *tu sudora* = to sweat, *sudoro* = sweating), and (3) to describe meteorological phenomena [*nive* = the snow, *tu niva* = to snow, *nivo* = snowing; *pluve* = the rain, *tu pluva* = to rain, *pluvo* = raining].

A fourth category of verbs may be derived in the same fashion, this group being described as cases in which no doubt about the meaning of the verb so derived is possible. This may clearly cover a very wide field. S. Auerbach gives two examples for this case [*parte* = the part, *tu parta* = to part, *parto* = parting; *honore* = the honour, *tu honora* = to honour, *honoro* = honouring]. Where the verb clearly indicates 'to provide with . . .' Novial uses the suffix -*is*- [Ido -*iz*-], [*krone* = the crown, *tu kron/is/a* = to crown, *kron/is/o* = crowning; *pipre* = the pepper, *tu pipr/is/a* = to pepper, *pipr/is/o* = peppering]. Verbs in -*a* cannot be derived directly from names of men or animals as -*a* is used to indicated the female sex. By adding '*tu*' to the infinitive of the verb Jespersen has added a further distinction to differentiate between noun and verb.

The solution which Jespersen has devised for the cases of direct derivation in Novial were made possible by the suppression of definite grammatical terminations for the various classes of words. Novial uses a great many affixes with precise meanings, which are in most cases identical with those of Ido.

VIII—3. Commentary

The problem of derivation cannot be said to have been finally solved by any of the existing systems. At the time of the delegation, Couturat's solution, based on the logical conception of the relationships of word families, seemed to some the ideal solution. It offered precision for the words so derived and apparently made Ido a more perfect instrument for use in science than any other system known before. But criticism was soon heard, being based on the difficulty of using correctly certain affixes, particularly -*if*-, -*ig*-, and -*iz*-. They were said to be difficult to master by the average student. Direct derivation in cases where these affixes should logically be used were easier for everyday use. Any departure from the logical conception of reversibility would destroy the logical structure of Ido and could therefore not be considered by Idists. Janis Roze has collected some interesting proposals in his *Report on the Decisions of the Interim Academy of Ido* (Riga, 1937). It was proposed to reduce the three affixes to their common denominator (-*i*-) for ordinary speech without necessarily suppressing the affixes—which had proved useful—for scientific terms. Thus -*i*- would stand for a variety of meanings and indicate that a more precise suffix had been replaced for the sake of ease. A number of proposals by S. Quarfood, Fr. Honoré, de Belie, and others, have been submitted for the sense for which -*i*- should stand. *Profet/o, profet/i/ar* = prophet, to prophesy; *filozof/o, filozof/i/ar* = philosopher, to philosophize; instead of *martel/agar* = to act with a hammer, *martel/i/ar* = to hammer, which would be the nearest approach to direct derivation without abandoning the principle of reversibility, analogically *fusiliar, kroniar*, etc. in the sense *to act with an instrument*. Alan Kelso has suggested deriving verbs directly from adjectives with the aid of -*i*-, *red/i/ar* = to make red, *net/i/ar* = to make clean, instead of *red/ig/ar* and *net/ig/ar*. No decisions have been taken on these proposals, but they may well be kept in mind for the question of derivation is not as yet finally settled for the planned language.

Another criticism has been raised against the derivation in Ido. *Dans*- is a verbal root in Ido and the noun directly derived [*dans/o*] expresses the act or state. In ethnic languages 'dance' may express either 'the action of dancing' or 'the dance' as an abstract designation. For common usage Ido has used the suffix -*ad*- to express the continued action, and the termination -*o* to describe the act or state, but this is not a purely logical solution. Other words belong to the same class, *parol/ar* = to speak, *parol/o* = speaking or speech, *pens/ar* = to think, *pens/o* = thinking or thought, *koncept/ar* = to conceive, *koncept/o* = conceiving or conception. The naturalists say that as perfect logicality in language cannot be achieved, the principle itself should be abandoned. It is questionable whether it is better to retain a few imperfections for which a better solution has yet to be found, or to reject the principle with which so many perfect forms can be obtained.

These problems are only briefly mentioned here to show that a profound comparative study will be required before the planned language can be fixed in its ultimate shape. If a linguistic commission decides that the planned language shall be formulated on autonomistic principles, *i.e.*, be precise and independent of the irregularities of ethnic tongues, the principles of Ido may be developed in the sense of the discussions and proposals sketched above. If, however, a more naturalistic solution is attempted, the principles offered by Occidental may be acceptable, *i.e.*, a development in close analogy to the Romanic languages, less precise but independent of the complications of a logically developed and coherent system of word derivation.

IX. Compounds and their Meaning

IX—1. Word composition in Esperanto

THE ETHNIC LANGUAGES USE compounds which are understood only by convention. No definite rule applies to their formation and usage alone defines their meaning. Esperanto has deliberately restricted its vocabulary to burden memory as little as possible, but to compensate for the lack of roots, the use of affixes and compounds is greater than in other constructed languages. Roots current in our daily language are made up in Esperanto of component parts to take the place of international roots. The disadvantage of this method is its lack of clarity. *ĝenerala popolvoĉdono* is the translation (*Français-Esperanto*) for E *plebiscite*. In the *Edinburgh Dictionary*, however, *plebiscito* is given as a neologism. Other terms formed analogically may be understood if well chosen but they are circumlocutions for which a shorter word is preferable. The compound *el-porti* is composed of *el* = out of, from among, fully, thoroughly and *porti* = to carry, to bear and is used to indicate 'to support'. The elements used in this combination do not make up the meaning of the new word, and the compound can thus be described as one of convention. *ĉirkaŭkrustaĵo* = that which is made of an outside crust, E *gangue*, Ido *gango*, is a type of word frequently to be found in Esperanto.

The limitations of a small vocabulary are mostly felt in the number of verbs and it is here that Esperanto uses compounds rather than international roots. Though these combinations are perfectly clear to an experienced Esperantist, they are purely artificial constructions to an outsider and it is precisely the outsider who should ultimately benefit by an auxiliary language.

The component parts of a coupled word should express the precise meaning for which the compound is used. If they are open to different interpretations they should not be admitted in a constructed language used by people accustomed to different linguistic habits. Compounds are unwieldy and are particularly unsuitable for scientific texts which depend on the highest possible precision. A scientific code could not rely on the use of compounds. Thousands of new roots would have to be chosen for the various nomenclatures and the principle of the selection of such roots and a regulated system or principle for the formation of compounds would be essential before an attempt is made to base a new code on a method which is haphazard and often illogical. The custom of liberally using compounds by convention is not in itself detrimental for everyday use, but some standard which is based on a wider vocabulary than that at present in existence in Esperanto, seems essential.

The principle followed in Esperanto is to distinguish between two parallel terminologies, (1) the *technical language* of the specialist and (2) the *ordinary language* of the non-specialist. The tendency is to adjust the known international terms to the spelling of Esperanto and to use them as purely technical terms [*fenikoptero*] and to use side by side the literal translation of non-technical language [*flamengo*, or *flambirdo*]. (*British Esperantist*, Sept.-Oct. 1945.)

IX—2. *Word composition in Ido*

The elements of Ido are monosignificant. The meaning of the compound is the resultant meaning of its elements and no compound should be formed, or used in analogy to ethnic languages, which contravenes this rule. In cases where Esperanto uses circumlocutions and where two Ido roots would not express the precise meaning which it is desired to express, Ido has introduced new roots. E *to impale* is expressed by the Ido root *empalar* while Esperanto uses a descriptive term *sidigi sur akrigita fosto* because no root has been sanctioned to express this meaning.

The compounds proper in Ido may be joined either with a hyphen [*post-marko*] or be written as one word [*postmarko*]. The grammatical termination of the first word may be omitted, or not [*fervoyo*, *vortilibri*]. The first word of a compound is always the determining element and the second the determined element [*fer-voyo* = railway, *mez-fingro* = middle finger]. Verbs may also form compounds [*tipo-skribar* = to typewrite; *manu-presar* = to shake hands]. The first noun, having the character of an adjectival attribute, may also accept this grammatical form [*post-marko* or *postala marko; resto-hemo*, or *restala hemo*].

In composition the ideas expressed in the elements are subject to a certain relationship. This relationship is not expressed in these compounds. *Motor-vehicle* is a vehicle propelled by a motor, a *railway* is a way of communication characterized by rails, a *house-key* is a key to open the door of a house, a *ring-finger* is a finger which carries the ring. This shows that the relationship of both elements in compounds is variable and is assumed to be understood, and it further shows that the greatest care should be employed in introducing new compounds. Two words may be joined together into a compound, and such a compound may be open to a different interpretation of the relationships of both words. Such compounds should not be used in a planned language, but a new word should be selected to cover the new term. Ambiguity in the constructed language must be avoided.

'A slap in the face' was rendered in earlier Esperanto writings as *survango* = on-the-cheek. The meaning of this compound is purely conventional as it cannot be logically deduced from its elements. It is abbreviated from the fuller *bato sur vango*, but in abbreviation eliminates the determining element (*bato*) retaining solely the determined element (*vango*) and the element indicating relationship (*sur*). In Ido the meaning is rendered more logically by *vango-frapo*, a form which has been accepted in Esperanto. 'To earn' is translated in Esperanto as *per-labori* = through working, which leaves out the essential determining element (earn) and retains only the determined element (work) and the element indicating the relationship (through or by). The newer form is the compound *labor-enspezi*, literally *work-receipt* which has acquired, by usage, the meaning *to earn*. This is inadmissible from the logical point of view. Ido renders this meaning by *ganar*, or more fully by *labor-ganar*. The progress in Esperanto towards simple international roots is slower than in Ido, though both meet, the one through usage and experience, the other through deliberate planning.

IX—3. *Word composition in Occidental*

Occidental has no fixed rule as to the use of compounds. It seems to follow the general usage of ethnic languages without having recourse to the artificial constructions of Esperanto and without limiting them to those logically understood. Occidental is in many ways a truer reflexion of the ethnic languages than any other constructed language and is inclined to admit usages and conventions of the Romanic group of languages.

The use of compounds in the planned language should be restricted, and is so restricted by the careful writer who has at his disposal the necessary linguistic material. The meaning of the compound should be the logical combination of the meaning of all elements; nothing should be assumed and nothing left to convention and usage.

X. Phonetic and Historic Spelling

In *Language, Its Nature, Development, and Origin* (chap. XXI, 9), Jespersen puts forward his theory on the general development of language and says that 'primitive language had a super-abundance of irregularities and anomalies. It was capricious and fanciful, and displayed a luxuriant growth of forms, entangled one with another like the trees in a primeval forest.' His conclusion on the growth of language is that it tends towards simplification, although this development is very slow. In every ethnic language a very gradual simplification of older forms has become apparent and spelling reform has either been deliberately attempted and furthered, or new forms are now displacing older ones by usage [E *labour* or *labor* new form used in America and Australia, *through* or *thru*; F *crystal*, new form *cristal; differentier*, new form *differencier; faquir*, new form *fakir* (decisions of the *Académie Française*) D *Concert*, new form *Konzert; Telephon*, new form *Telefon; That* new form *Tat*].

For the purpose of a planned auxiliary language, two schools of thought have developed, respectively called the autonomistic and the naturalistic school. Zamenhof introduced into Esperanto the principle of one letter for each sound. Ido accepted this principle but adopted the West-European alphabet and therefore admitted some well-known letters, not contained in the Esperanto alphabet [*x, y, q(u), w*]; these were required for the easier recognition of many words [*exempl/o* rather than *ekzempl/o*]. Both languages, however, use a more or less phonetic system of spelling. If we accept Jespersen's assumption of a gradual progress towards simpler forms of the ethnic languages, the principle of phonetic spelling in a planned language would be justified, as it anticipates the general linguistic development. The obsolete forms of living languages would no longer be an argument for accepting historic spelling.

Occidental, Latino sine flexione and, to some extent, Novial, represent the so-called naturalistic school of thought. They have not accepted the principle of phonetic spelling. Their aim is to discover and bring into a regulated system the present-day usages of ethnic languages. In saying that Novial represents, to some extent, the

naturalistic school, it should be said that Novial started originally as
a phonetic system and that only after six years Jespersen introduced
an alternative system of spelling. Since then he differentiated between *Phonetic Novial* (F.N. 1928) and *Orthographic Novial* (O.N.
1934). In the following paragraph the differences in theory and
practical application of both schools are shown.

X—1. *Sound and letter*

The autonomistic systems have aimed at a complete phonetic
system of spelling, Esperanto using six new supersigned letters [ĉ, ĝ,
ĥ, ĵ, ŝ, ŭ], in analogy to Russian sounds, while Ido uses the Latin
alphabet. This principle has been carried through irrespective of the
historic spelling in ethnic languages. The vowels [a, e, i, o, u]
represent one sound only in both languages. Their pronunciation
should be of medium length, *a* as in *father*, *e* as in *veil*, *i* as in
machine, *o* as in *glory*, *u* as in *rule*. The value of the vowel is never
influenced by the consonant following it or by the doubling of such
consonant.

The naturalistic systems differentiate between long and short
vowels, and they add one vowel to the alphabet (*y*, in Occidental
with the value of the French *u*, in Orthographic Novial with the
value of *i*), using *y* both as vowel and consonant. Vowels in syllables
not stressed are short. Stressed vowels followed by a double consonant are short. All other vowels are long with the exception of a
number of prepositions [*con, de, in, per,* etc.].

X—2. *Double consonants*

The autonomistic systems do not admit double consonants. The
naturalistic systems admit double consonants [*rr, ss, tt,* etc.] for
several functions, (1) to shorten the preceding vowel [*lettre*], (2) to
follow the historic spelling of the ethnic languages [*necessi, gazette*],
(3) for the purpose of flexion [*curre/r, cur/s*] the second root -*r* preceding -*e* being changed into -*s* according to de Wahl's rule.

Two arguments are put forward against double consonants, (1) in
the autonomistic systems a double consonant would serve no useful
purpose, as all vowels are pronounced with even length, (2) the
spelling of some words with double consonants and of others with
single consonants would be an unnecessary burden to memory.

In some cases the double consonant serves to distinguish two
roots. Here the autonomistic systems had to change the root slightly,
while the naturalistic languages were able to express the difference
through the double consonant, or in some cases through a different
ending :

E	earth	to frighten, noun: terror
Occ.	terra	terrer
Esp.	tero	teruri
Ido	tero	terorar

X—3. c, k, and other letters

The autonomistic systems transcribe the sound 'k' always with the letter *k* [E *electrification*, Ido *elektrifik/o*], the naturalistic systems retain the historic spelling [Occ. *electrifica/t/ion*].

The consonants *c, s, z* have one defined function in the autonomistic systems, *c* is pronounced as *ts;* *s* as in *house*, always sharp or unvoiced, *z* as in *organize*, always soft or voiced [*cent, savar, rozo*]. The naturalistic systems follow the ethnic languages and pronounce *c* as *k* before *a, o, u*, and before other consonants or at the end of the word, but as *ts* before *e, i, y* [*decimal-classification*]; *s* generally voiced between two vowels, but unvoiced if double *ss* [*proposir, cession*], sharp in all other cases [*sestra* = sister]; *z* as *ds*, and *zz* as *ts*.

The letter *g* of the autonomistic school is always pronounced as in *gold*, with the exception of the accented letter [ĝ] in Esperanto. The naturalists give it the value of a hard *g* as in *gold* before *a, o, u*, and consonants, and a soft *g* as in *general* before *e, i, y*. The *t* in Occidental is pronounced as *ts* if followed by *ie, ia*, or *io* [*genera/t/ion*], it retains its usual value in all other cases [*senti/r* = to feel]. Ido uses respectively *c* or *t* [*generacion/o, sent/ar*].

Jespersen has solved the problem in his original Phonetic Novial in a different way. On the whole he follows the pattern of the autonomistic systems, but proposes a different treatment of the letter *c*. This letter has caused much discussion and disagreement because it is internationally well-known as representing three sounds, *k, ts,* and *s*. Jespersen writes instead of the *c, k* or *s* according to circumstances [E *circle*, Nov. *sirkle*, E *occident*, Nov. *oksidente*]. He discards the letter *z* completely and adopts the usage of the ethnic languages, *s* with voiced sound between vowels [E *to organize, to excuse*, Nov. *exkuso*]. In 1934 Jespersen divided his language into the so-called F.N. (phonetic Novial), as originally planned, and O.N. (orthographic Novial). In the latter he used the letters *c; ç* (before *a, o, u*); and *sc; y* (pronounced as *i*), and *z*. Although he still believed *k* and *s* to be the more rational solution, he respected the customs of the non-phonetical world in admitting these letters. He was certain that, had he written from the beginning *central, zone, systeme* instead of *sentral, sone, sisteme*, his language would have met with more success.

X—4. International consonants and digraphs

Esperanto has followed phonetic spelling strictly to the extent of using new symbols, while Ido has only admitted the letters of the Latin alphabet. Ido has accepted two digraphs [*ch, sh*] as they are known in the European languages, although they each represent one sound only. To be consistent, Zamenhof has accepted *ĉ, ŝ* to represent these sounds. For the soft sound of *g* Esperanto uses the supersigned letter [ĝ] while Ido insisted on the hard pronunciation of *g* in *general/a* and, for certain words, has altered the spelling into *j* [*jer/ant/o*, F gérant].

A comparison of the main differences gives us the following table:

Esp. kv — ks kz f t ĉ ŝ g ĝ ĵ j   ĥ (guttural)
Occ. qu w x — ph t(h) ch sh g g j y (consonant)—
Ido qu w x — f t   ch sh g j j y   —

Esperanto is the only planned language that uses new supersigns which alter the value of the consonant. Occidental uses the supersign [*hom*/*an*/*it*/*à*] only to indicate stress where it deviates from its rules of pronunciation. Ido uses the letters *q, w, x, y,* and the two digraphs *ch, sh,* to depart as little as possible from the European languages, and in such a way that these letters do not contravene its rules of pronunciation.

Owing to their close adherence to the ethnic languages, the naturalistic systems have been able to maintain the historic and international spelling of chemical elements and their abbreviations, as well as the spelling and abbreviations of terms of other nomenclatures. The autonomistic systems translate the names of these elements and terms according to their own rules (Esperanto rule 15, *Plena gramatiko de Esperanto, Fundamenta Krestomatio,* pp. 254-256). They have, however, made the concession of retaining the international symbols [*Cl* = *kloro; Ca* = *kalcio*]. Laurent, in his *La Langue Internationale Ido et son application aux sciences pharmacologiques* gives a table of ninety chemical elements. The symbol varies from any possible contraction of the Ido translation of each element in eighteen cases out of ninety, a comparatively small proportion.

X—5. *Some arguments on phonetic spelling*

The naturalistic school advances several reasons for their historic form of spelling and we shall examine them carefully. They admit that the rules of pronunciation, when such spelling is used, are more difficult, but, they say, millions of people already know these word forms. The greater difficulty in spelling is compensated by the recognition at first sight of the forms already known.

Two objections can be made to this argument. If the naturalists assume that the international word forms are known to millions of people, they must be thinking either of people who have a polyglot smattering or knowledge, or of people having one of the Romanic languages as their mother tongue. The number of persons having a polyglot knowledge is small, and excludes the greater part of the people who will ultimately benefit by a planned language. They must further assume that scientists, technicians, and economists will of necessity continue to learn one or several ethnic languages. Clearly, the object of a planned language is to do away with the necessity of learning ethnic languages, to do away with spending years to master the irregularities of these languages for sciences for which a knowledge of them is not directly required. A medical man, or a technician, should not be asked to spend years of his time in studying foreign languages which are of no immediate help to his profession, as soon as a planned language makes available to him all the literature and dissertations which he must read. The planned language will in the future fulfil the function which the acquisition of one or two foreign languages has never been able to satisfy: it will open the way to international communication without requiring many valuable years of study. If the argument of greater facility in recognizing known forms is correct for people who have one of the Romanic languages as their mother tongue, we should recall the admirable dictum of Jespersen that that language is best which is easiest for the greatest number. If it could be proved that existing international forms are preferable to regularity of structure, then the solution offered by the naturalistic school should be adopted.

The naturalists further say that, as long as the main languages of Europe maintain their imperfect spelling, the planned language has no reason to do otherwise. As soon as the ethnic languages decide to adopt phonetic spelling, the planned language can follow these changes.

German, Spanish, French, and other languages have been reformed in the direction of phonetic simplification but so far Occidental has not taken these changes into account. A number of words are spelled in Occidental either with single or double consonants [*difuse/r, diffuse/r*], in which the double consonant should shorten the preceding vowel. In French, however, this rule does not apply [F *terre, flamme*] but Occidental still retains the historic spelling of French by writing *terra*, it retains visual facility but sacrifices the known sound of the word. A further objection to historic spelling is the difficulty of memorizing the correct forms. Even if we do depart from the supposedly known forms of the ethnic languages we cannot always arrive at a common form, for the spelling may differ considerably [FE *race*, D *Rasse*, I *razza*, S *raza;* FE *connexion* (but to connec*t*), E *eccentric*, F *excentrique;* E *ecstasy*, F *extase*].

The double function of *c* and of *t* enable Occidental to retain the historic spelling and yet to pronounce the words according to ethnic usages [*public, public/a/tion, public/ità*]. Affixes beginning with *i* influence the pronunciation but not the spelling. Before a suffix beginning with *e*, however, the pronunciation is maintained and the word or the endings are modified [*amic* but *amic/os* instead of *amic/es; seg* but *seg/as* instead of *seg/es;* but *seg-h/eria*, the *h* modifying the pronunciation of *g*].

XI. Logic and Accepted Convention

XI—1. The logic of relationship

THE TERM 'LOGIC' IN relation to language is open to different interpretations. The logicality to which Couturat referred in a planned system of language was not the Aristotelian logic of genus or species, but rather the logic of relationship which determines the functions of the elements of speech. Logicality requires the simple principle that each element of this language has, as far as practicable, one invariable meaning which it retains in all connexions. Logicality further requires that irregular forms be excluded. If the system fulfils both these demands we can then formulate the rule of reversibility. Logicality thus is the composite result of monosignificance, regularity, and reversibility. Reversibility covers a set of rules which allows of an analysis of all derived forms and compounds and by which we can return to the original root or roots of a word. It follows that the logicality of which we are speaking in relation to language, is the logic of common sense which is not a hidden quality, but a feature which can be incorporated in a planned and constructed system of language.

Let us return to the problems of derivation to make this principle quite clear. We will have to restrict ourselves to the autonomistic systems, and in particular to Ido, as the naturalistic systems reject, more or less, the application of logic.

The words of the language consist of invariable elements of three kinds, roots, affixes, and grammatical terminations. The roots can be divided into two groups, verbal roots expressing a state, or action [*labor, parol, konstrukt*], and nominal or substantival roots denoting an object (living being or thing), or expressing an aspect of it [*person, garden, bel, blind*]. The verbal root can produce directly a verb or noun expressing the state or action [*laborar* = to work, *laboro* = the work; *parolar* = to speak, *parolo* = speech; *konstruktar* = to construct, *konstrukto* = constructing]. The grammatical termination [*-ar, -o, -a, -e*] determines only the grammatical function of the root. The meaning of the root is retained throughout all derivatives.

If we wish to apply the rules of logical relationship to the planned language, the meaning of the words must not be arbitrary or be fixed by convention only. If *labor/ar* means to work, *labor/o* can not mean either the worker or the work. If we wish to express another idea not implied in the root, we must add to the root an affix which carries this idea in this case and in all analogical cases [*labor-* = work-, *labor/ist/o* = work-er]. The use of such an affix, or any other affix, does not change the fundamental meaning of the root. Its modifying purpose is to add the meaning of the affix to that of the root. In consequence of this rule, adopted by Couturat for Ido, he formulated the principle of reversibility which enables us always to determine the original root by a simple analysis of the derivative which may consist of a root, a prefix, and one or more suffixes.

If we start from the verbal root [*labor-*] the noun directly derived can only express the action or state expressed by the verb [*labor/o* = the work]. In ethnic languages the verbal noun is often reproduced in the form of the infinitive [F *le manger, le boire, le dormir, le rire;* D *das Rennen, das Essen, das Lachen*]. English uses the infinitive with the ending *-ing* for this purpose.

What is the relationship between a nominal root and the adjective derived from it? If *blind/a* means blind, *blind/o* must mean a person or thing that is of the quality . . . = a blind person, *bel/a* = beautiful, *bel/o* = a beautiful person.

In Ido the present indicative is characterized by *-a-*, the past indicative by *-i-*, and the future indicative by *-o-* [*me drinkas, me drinkis, me drinkos*]. The three tenses are always indicated by these three vowels. The active and passive participles submit to it [*konvinkata, konvinkanta; konvinkita, konvinkinta; konvinkota, konvinkonta*], and it is, logically, also extended to the infinitive [*drinkar, drinkir, drinkor*]. In practice, the past and future infinitive will seldom be used and there is very little necessity to teach these forms in the early lessons of a grammar. They are, however, possible and can express fine shades of meaning. The fact that they exist shows that the characteristics of the three tenses have been logically carried through the whole system of conjugation to a greater extent than in any other system.

Louis Couturat is generally considered the originator of the introduction of logicality into the planned language. The Delegation had accepted the principle of monosignificance which was the basis of the rule of reversibility. He defended these principles in *Étude sur la dérivation* and *International Language and Science*, saying that 'the international language borrows its *stems* from the European languages according to the principle of maximum internationality, *i.e.*, it adopts for each idea the most international stem, namely, that which is familiar to the greatest number of men. It cannot, and must not, borrow their derivatives from living languages without losing all its theoretical and practical advantages, because the natural derivatives are too irregular. Sometimes the same affix has several different meanings, sometimes the same relationship is expressed by different affixes. . . . The international language must be autonomous in its formation of words; when the elements which it borrows from our languages have once been chosen (in the best possible manner), it must combine them freely according to its own rules, preserving their invariable form and monosignificant meaning.'

This then is the meaning of the logic of relationship as the autonomists conceive it and one which reduces the problem of word formation to a few simple rules.

XI—2. *The choice of affixes*

The principle of logicality requires a complement, namely, the satisfactory selection of the elements (roots and affixes). Much criticism on the selection and meaning of these affixes has been made. In many cases the affixes of Esperanto and Ido are identical and it may be sufficient to examine more closely those of Ido as they always conform to the principle of reversibility, *i.e.*, they indicate the same relationship of the root to the full word.

Otto Jespersen in *An International Language* criticizes some affixes and asks how can we translate into Ido D Resultat, as *rezulto*, *rezultajo* or *rezulturo?* Is D logisch = *logikala* or *logikoza?* If *nivar* means to snow, then *nivo* should mean the act of snowing, and *nivajo* or *nivuro* = snow. It is quite true that in Ido we have, in certain cases, to select between several affixes. A 'logical conclusion' may be *logikoza konkluzo* = a conclusion full of logic, or *logikala konkluzo* = a conclusion related to logic. *Derivato*, the noun formed from the passive participle [*derivata*] may be used besides *derivajo* = the object possessing the quality of the original word, or *derivuro* denoting the result of the act of the verbal root.

We have previously seen that logic can only be applied to the extent practicable, and Couturat reminds us in his *Étude* that by a natural and unavoidable extension, of which the ethnic languages constantly give examples, the noun immediately derived from a verb means the action as well as the essential and immediate result of the action, the idea of which is often inseparable from the action itself.

A further criticism of the series of verbs ending in *-esas* has been advanced by R. Berger. The root of the auxiliary verb *esar* [*es-*] is used to form the passive infinitive [*punis/ar* = to punish, *punis/es/ar* = to be punished]. Berger says that logically the passive voice should be formed with the passive participle and not the infinitive, which would give us the form *punis/at/esar*.

Ido would have become a purely philosophical language, an *a priori* system, if de Beaufront, Couturat, and the delegation had attempted to make it rigidly logical. That rigid logic was rejected by Couturat. Logicality was restricted to the extent practicable and, although it was well recognized that it cannot be the rigid logic of the Greek philosophers, practical logic remained the best basis on which an easy and regular artificial language could be constructed. The quality regarded as important was not merely ease but ease and clarity.

Matejka gives two interesting justifications for the application of logic to a constructed language (*Progreso*, ix, 91-92), (1) The child which learns its mother tongue shows an instinctive tendency to form words according to the laws of analogy and regularity. This analogy exists precisely in the application of the laws of logic and is not an analogy which copies the irregularities of the ethnic languages. (2) In learning foreign languages the student makes many mistakes because he follows his natural tendency of trying to make the language conform to logical forms. This proves, according to Matejka, that logicality has deep roots in our mental life.

Whether we choose in Ido the form *logikala*, *logikoza* or *logika*, or even *segunlogika* is of little consequence as long as the sense of the sentence is clear. In this connexion we may be reminded of Couturat's maxim that 'the sentence is the smallest unit of thought.' The person who wishes to choose each expression meticulously may prefer one form to another of possible translations. For the case quoted by Jespersen and Berger [*niv/ar, niv/o; punis/at/esar*] the authors of Ido made a concession to conventional abbreviations, as Berger puts it. So far, however, the critics could not suggest a better solution which would fit into the system of practicable logicality.

XI—3. *The naturalistic school and logicality*

Esperanto bases its derivation on the rule of necessity and sufficiency, words derive their meaning from the meaning of their component parts and—to some extent—from the context; Ido on logicality to the extent practicable (monosignificance, regularity, reversibility); and Occidental, the outstanding naturalistic system, on usage *i.e.*, convention and analogy. This analogy is not based on logical conceptions but on the analogy of irregular and arbitrary forms (see the use of the suffix *-ion*).

The naturalists say that language is far too complex to conform to some rigid rules based on logicality, that we cannot attain strictly monosignificant forms in a constructed language because that implies a vocabulary of such dimensions that it would become quite impracticable for everyday use. As Ido has, admittedly, not been able to achieve perfect but only practicable logicality, the naturalists say that a constructed language should not choose logic at all. Logic, as applied to language, has at least four elements (*Cosmoglotta*, Doc. 172), (1) regularity, (2) monosignificance, (3) reversibility, (4) elimination of ambiguity. *Cosmoglotta* asserts that most of these inherent qualities summarized under the heading of logicality cannot be attained, and should not form the basis of a language.

The differences of the autonomistic and the naturalistic schools are due to the fact that both depart from opposite premises. The autonomists regard logicality as an indispensable factor to the achievement of clarity and ease of learning, while the naturalists reject the principle and follow far more closely the pattern of the existing ethnic or 'natural' languages. They base their system on the internationality of words and elements, defining internationality as the 'foreknowledge of international forms'.

Convention and analogy to naturalists mean forms which are in current use in several ethnic languages. When this cannot be achieved with a single invariable affix, several affixes may be used to describe the same relationship. Thus Occidental uses *-tà, -ie, -ess, -ntie* in place of the affix *-eso* in Ido [*amabilità, maladie, finess, ignorantie*]. In some cases this gives rise to parallel forms [*povress* and *povrità; amicità* and *amicie*]. Occidental further distinguishes between *yuness* = youth, the state of being young; *yunità* quality of being young; and *yunité* = youth in a collective sense. The term for childhood cannot be analogically formed as *infantess* but is rendered as *infantie*. Similar uncertainty is experienced with the suffixes *-er, -atu, -ore, -agie, -ment, -ura*, etc. The variety of affixes which may be used does not always lead to the true international form, as Jespersen was able to show [*scrition, analysation, interprension* = enterprise, *descrovition*]. These forms have no equivalents in existing languages.

The difference between the two schools is a difference of principle. Ido departs from invariable elements composed according to definite rules; Occidental departs from the full words of the ethnic languages which are already internationally known. Although we may, in some cases, have a choice in Ido between affixes which express slightly different shades of meaning [*logikala, logikoza, segunlogika*] each word so formed is grammatically correct. In Occidental a word formed from a root and an affix with a definition which fits the case may be grammatically incorrect because it is unnatural [*capital/ario* = capitalist, *prolitar/ité* = proletariat]. The analogy applied in Occidental is one to already existing forms. It is not an analogy to forms regularly and autonomically arrived at.

IALA's criteria of 1937 (research directives which are still under discussion) propose that the structural features of the language shall be logical, regular, and autonomous. The commentary shows the difference of principle in Esperanto, Ido, and Occidental, a question which has been more fully treated in Chapter XII. In conclusion we may say that the naturalists have achieved, on the whole, forms which are more international and therefore more easily understood at first view. The autonomists have obtained more regular forms which are more precise and less dependent on the forms of ethnic languages. The latter are easier to compose once the rules of derivation have been mastered, while Occidental requires the knowledge of several ethnic languages to arrive at the correct words, or, inversely, a longer study of the ethnic languages to arrive at the forms which should be used in Occidental.

XII. Autonomistic and Naturalistic Principles

XII—1. Points of departure

THE RESPECTIVE MERITS OF the autonomistic and naturalistic schools of thought for the planned language can be assessed only if we know their different points of departure. A mere comparison of the forms and rules without a knowledge of divergent and sometimes opposing principles will not give a fair picture of either type of language. The autonomistic school is mainly represented by the two systems Esperanto and Ido; the naturalistic school is mainly represented by the two systems Occidental and Interlingua (Latino sine flexione). Novial is based on autonomistic principles but contains some naturalistic features, and can thus be described as an intermediate system between the two schools of thought.

The guiding principle of the naturalists is the closest possible similarity to existing forms of the ethnic languages, and preferably to the Romanic group of languages. The elements and forms shall be natural. Immediate comprehensibility is more important than forms independent (*autonomistic*) of the existing languages and any factor contributing to naturalness is desirable.

The autonomists demand that all elements (roots and affixes) shall be monosignificant and independent (*autonomous*) of the existing languages even though they are modelled—to the extent practicable —on these languages. All elements shall be monosignificant and be related to each other in a logical manner; they shall be independent of all conventional usages (*irregular collocations*—Palmer). The rules and elements shall be regular (without exceptions).

XII—2. Words and affixes

In consequence of these principles, the naturalists set out from the full words in the ethnic languages which are in international use, *i.e.*, common to several European languages. The affixes selected were defined according to the meaning which they have in ethnic languages, and which may vary in different connexions. The definitions of affixes are, of necessity, wide, general, and not precise [-*ion* denoting action, state, or results]. De Wahl and Peano thus achieved a nearer approach to natural forms than did the authors of the auto-nomistic systems.

Esperanto and Ido chose their elements from the ethnic languages but assigned one function only to each element (root or affix). The result was a more regular system and greater precision of the terms, and, in Ido, the application of reversibility of all derivatives. Its obvious disadvantage was a greater artificiality of many forms in the language [Ido-Esp. *delegitaro*, Occ. *delegation*].

To absorb as many international expressions as possible, de Wahl was obliged to take from the ethnic languages many more affixes than either Esperanto or Ido. In Chapter III only the most important ones are enumerated. In some cases we have a choice of four or more affixes but unless we know the international or conventional form as used in the ethnic languages, we cannot autonomously apply it with the help of definite rules [*yuness* but *infantie*]. We may know the root and a number of affixes which, according to their definitions, may be equally correct. Even analogy to other forms in Occidental does not always lead to the correct form. Further still, the many affixes from which we may select the correct one—either by previous know-ledge of the ethnic base languages, or by an imitation of good writers in Occidental—does not always lead to an international form, for even a wide choice of affixes must still be limited in a constructed language [*interprension* = enterprise, *descovrition*, etc.].

XII—3. Spelling

The naturalists have consistently followed the principle of natural-ness and have adopted the so-called historic (or etymological) spell-ing. They have justified it by saying that as soon as phonetic spelling is adopted in the ethnic languages, their system will follow. However, for aesthetic reasons they accept the present usage of ethnic languages rather than anticipating such simplification. The authors of the naturalistic systems have retained double consonants, the double pronunciation of *c*, *g* and *t*, the use of *y* as a consonant and a vowel. They have retained the use of accents for stress and in some few cases for differentiation of meaning [*in* accented has the negative meaning of non or un, *inscrit* = unwritten; *in* unaccented has the meaning of E in, *inscrit* = written in]. Either the grave accent [`] or the acute accent ['] may be used for stress [*logicalità*].

The autonomists have tried, as far as practicable, to adopt phonetic spelling. Ido has compromised by retaining *x* and *q*, *sh* and *ch*. Esperanto has suppressed *x* and *q* and substituted *ks* or *kz* for *x*. Double consonants were suppressed and each letter has one function only.

In adopting historic spelling de Wahl was able to retain the known abbreviations of chemical formulae in Occidental. Ido had to make a concession to science by retaining the known formulae, which were not, however, the natural abbreviations of the terms in Ido.

XII—4. *Indicative endings*

The autonomistic systems have a number of terminations which serve to indicate the grammatical species of the words. [*-o, -a, -e,* etc.] .The argument in favour of these endings is that they help the student to identify the component parts of a phrase more easily. They are an important factor for ease of learning of the planned language.

Rather than follow the accepted grammatical pattern of noun in singular and plural, adjective, adverb and the tenses, some Esperanto teachers have accepted a simplification, and refer to various word classes as the *-o group* which indicates an object, the *-a group* which indicates a quality, the *-e group* which indicates how a thing is done, etc. They thus avoid the necessity of referring to grammatical terms which offer difficulties to some students.

The naturalistic systems reject these obligatory endings which they call pleonastic, *i.e.,* superfluous. It is argued that if suffixes are added to words which end in either *-o* or *-a* etc., these endings are superfluous because they do not fulfil any derivative function. They are considered *a priori* designs for certain classes of words which have no parallel in any ethnic language. These endings, they say, are unnatural and have, by their repetition in writing and speech, a bad effect on style. Occidental does, however, admit such pleonastic endings in certain cases, and these endings have to be suppressed if a suffix is added [*hom(e), homanità; fat/e, fat/al*]. In Occidental it is necessary to remember which letter is part of the root and which is simply added as a pleonastic ending. In Ido and Esperanto the grammatical ending is always retained and follows the suffix or suffixes, *i.e.,* the suffix or suffixes are inserted between root and grammatical termination [*labor/ar* = to work, *labor/o* = the work, *labor/ant/o* = the worker)].

For aesthetic reasons the naturalists object to the use of *-a* to denote the adjective. In Spanish *-a* denotes the feminine gender, and, say the naturalists, the phrase *la bona patro* = the good father, would be objectionable to people accustomed to *-a* for the feminine, and *-o* for the masculine.

Occidental admits the optional *-i* for adjectives and the optional *-e* for nouns. The plural ending is *-s,* and *-e* is then required [*hom(e)* = man, *homes* = men; *par(e)* = pair, *pares* = pairs].

The demand for euphony is often used as an argument in favour of the endings of Esperanto and Ido. The vowel endings of Ido, and to a lesser degree Esperanto, make them similar in sound to Italian.

XII—5. *Analytic and synthetic conjugation*

Esperanto and Ido use the so-called synthetic form of conjugation as well as the analytic conjugation with the auxiliary verb *esti* or *esar.* Occidental and Novial use the analytic form, *i.e.,* with auxiliary verbs [Occ. *yo ha amat,* Nov. *me did ama,* Ido *me amabis* or *me esis amanta*]. Jespersen introduced the analytic form besides the simple past as a useful alternative. It should not be used with the same emphatic meaning as in present-day English, but rather as an alternative for the simple past, as in Elizabethan English when *he did say* meant nothing more than *he said*. The *-ab-* [*am-ab-is*] forms in Ido are very rarely used as the simple past expresses the idea adequately in most cases. S. Quarfood (*La Akademio*) has proposed some new forms of analytic conjugation for Ido but they have, so far, not been accepted. These proposals show, however, that analytic conjugation could well be fitted into the structure of Ido or Esperanto if interlinguistic experiments proved them to be desirable.

PART III

XIII. The Preliminary Project for a Technical Nomenclature of the Soviet-Russian Academy of Sciences

XIII—1. A brief history of technical terminology

THE ABSENCE OF AN agreed international technical terminology has seriously impeded or made more difficult technical developments. This fact was recognized and valuable preparatory work for the creation of a nomenclature of technology began some years ago. The following paragraphs trace this development from its beginnings in 1927.

The International Federation of the National Standardizing Associations (ISA) was founded in 1926. The International Electrotechnical Commission (IEC) had done considerable research and preparatory work for the simplification of the international electrotechnical code which was begun about 20 years earlier. While the IEC dealt exclusively with the electrotechnical side of the problem, the ISA undertook to work for a solution of the code problem for all other sciences. The ISA initiated in 1931 the publication of a comprehensive survey including the use of an international planned language as a possible solution. The general meeting, held in 1932, of the German Federation of the Societies of Technical Sciences, as well as the Soviet-Russian Standardizing Commission, took up this question. The Soviet-Russian Commission suggested in 1934 that the ISA should begin to work for a code of the technical sciences, similar in application to the botanical and zoological nomenclatures which are based on Latin. A similar proposal had been submitted as early as 1927 by the Japanese Commission.

In May 1934 the Soviet-Russian proposal was circulated to all the national standardizing commissions by ISA. A conference, held in September 1934 in Stockholm, considered a very full report on the subject. This was submitted by the Soviet-Russian Standardizing Commission and was edited by Ernst Drezen, the chairman of the section for nomenclatures of the Soviet-Russian Standardizing Commission. The report was fully approved by the Commission for Terminology of the Soviet-Russian Academy of Sciences.

The report has since been published in Esperanto. Its six main chapters summarize the contents, (1) International relations and

Latin, (2) Historic development of technical-scientific definitions, terms, and symbols, (3) Technical-scientific classification as a condition for the unification of definitions and terms, (4) International symbols and systems, (5) National standardization of technical terms, (6) International standardization of technical terms. This report, according to Wüster (*Sparwirtschaft*, I, 1936) was unanimously accepted by the representatives of nineteen national standardizing associations.

XIII—2. *The detailed second report*

After the first report had been so favourably received, the Soviet-Russian Standardizing Commission formed a special committee for the preparation of a code project. This committee was composed of Ernst Drezen, Professor Chatelin, one of the leading figures in electrotechnical science in Soviet-Russia, Professor Spielrein, electrotechnician and formerly assistant lecturer at the Technical College in Stuttgart, Professor Shirkov, a philologist, all being consultant members of the Soviet-Russian Academy of Sciences. The final report, discussed here, was examined and revised by the committee on terminology of the Academy of Sciences.

In June 1935 ISA circularized the national standardizing associations with the English version of the report. A German translation was issued in November for the German speaking countries and a French version was sent to affiliated organizations of the Latin countries.

The report is a fairly comprehensive review of the problems, the proposed solutions, and the scope of the code. Three main principles are suggested for the structure of the code, (1) the principle of greatest internationality in form and content of the elements of the code and their connexions, (2) facility in applying the code, short terms, facility in memorizing the terms, ease of pronunciation, simplicity and ease in forming derivatives and compounds, clarity of the words, intelligibility, (3) precision of meaning. The code should not include any elements which are not perfectly clear. In this connexion it is recommended to profit by the experiences of the planned languages Esperanto, Ido, Occidental, and Novial.

The authors mention that at the moment the following organizations are dealing with the question of terminological standardization —the International Commission for Measures and Weights (CIPM), the International Electrotechnical Commission (IEC), the International Commission for Lighting and Electrical Equipment (IBK), the Advisory Council for International Telecommunications, and others. All these groups working for the solution of a scientific nomenclature for their particular section should be consulted by the ISA which is to prepare the way for the terminological code. To facilitate the work they propose to begin with those sections which belong to the exact sciences and to continue with chemistry, electrotechnics, geology, mineralogy, botanics, and zoology. The definition of terms for the production of machine tools, for architecture and structional terms will prove more difficult and the proper selection of the word-building elements and the rules of application are of particular importance.

XIII—3. *The grammar of the proposed code*

The alphabet proposed is the Latin one. This has found widest acceptance and should be based, as far as possible, on phonetic principles without the introduction or use of diacritic signs. The authors advocate a solution as in Esperanto, *i.e.*, in cases in which Latin is unable to reproduce certain sounds phonetically. As an alternative accent to the Esperanto sign [^] they suggest ᵛ, used in some Slav languages, for the letters *c, g, j, s.* The accented *h* [ĥ] is suppressed and instead of ĵ, an alternative solution [ĝ] is suggested. According to Professor I. Hermann, the Advisory Council for International Telecommunications (CCIF) has accepted the Esperanto alphabet for fixing syllables used in testing far-distant cables.

The main elements of the code are the word-roots. The code will have to contain technical and common roots. The common roots [*head, screw, resistance, power*] would have to be selected according to their greatest internationality and ease of learning and they may be used as component parts of technical terms. Compounds would have to be part of the code [*screw-head, aero-drome*], although theoretically one could introduce new terms for them and attain greater precision. But this could only be done at the expense of the facility of learning and memorizing the new terms. The various international technical terms are subdivided into nine groups, for each of which three examples are quoted as an illustration. (1) mathematical terms [*aksiom, ekstrapol, hipotez*], (2) arithmetical [*absolut, adici, bikvadrat*], (3) metrical measurements [*metr, gram, ton*], (4) algebraical [*binom, ekvivalent, koeficient*], (5) geometrical [*angul, baz, cilindr*], (6) trigonometrical [*kosinus, kotangent, sekant*], (7) higher mathematical [*analitik, cikloid, elips*], (8) mechanical [*centrifug, diaterm, dinamik*], (9) physical [*amplitud, frekvenc, magnetism*]. The above examples are spelt as in the report and are obviously based on Esperanto.

A list of about 1,000 terms of a technical and general nature is proposed, of which most are already known to the scientist as they are used with little or no variation in the European languages. The authors assume that by admitting compounds and a fairly unrestricted derivation, the thousand roots would be sufficient to cover most technical terms.

The 24 prepositions and conjunctions are mainly taken from Esperanto with a few alternative forms from Ido [*vice, cirkum, ed, kontre, maksimum*].

With the exception of eight affixes, the complete list proposed is taken from Esperanto with their original meaning. Six of the eight exceptions are taken from Ido [*mis-, retro-, -end, -iv, -iz, -oz*]. The two others are taken from scientific terms, *hiper-* denoting excess [*hiper/satur/ig/i*], *-oid* denoting analogy in form and aspect [*ŝton/oid/a*].

The grammar of the code is restricted to a minimum, containing only 18 rules, mainly based on the grammar of Esperanto. The rule for the formation of compounds is based on linguistic usage, often open to different interpretation. The grammatical terminations are to be optional.

XIV. Technology and the Language Problem

XIV—1. Technical Terminology

THE PROBLEMS CONFRONTING TECHNICIANS who set out to create a code of technical terms were different from those facing a group of linguists who wish to create a planned auxiliary language. The problems to be solved are limited by the scope of such a code. The demands made on the code will finally decide whether anything short of a complete grammatical system and a fixed vocabulary will be adequate. International and universal use is the purpose of such a terminology. This makes it necessary to study its many problems, its construction, and its composition with an impartial approach and a full knowledge of recent linguistic and interlinguistic developments. ISA (International Federation of the National Standardizing Associations) has begun an independent study of these problems and Dr E. Wüster reported in 1936 to ISA, at a conference in Budapest (Committee ISA 37, terminology). This chapter summarizes the points of the report. Remarks and comments have been added where it seemed that this would contribute to their further clarification.

The code shall be able to incorporate fully all systems of international terminology already in use, and in such a form as is recognizably near to the original system. The code should be so formed that it can easily be adapted to new fields. The code words shall be spelled and pronounced in the same manner in all countries.

XIV—2. International words

What are the common features of so-called 'international words' and in what way do they differ? (1) The word *energy* differs but slightly in the European languages, though its pronunciation varies. In English it is spelled with *y*, in French with *ie*, in German with a capital *E* and *ie*, in Spanish with *ia*. (2) The word *abies*, in botanical science, is spelled in the same manner in all countries. Its pronunciations differs in these countries. (3) The word *shunt* is spelled and pronounced in the same manner in all countries. The first class of words is the most common in persent terminologies. The words comprising the technical code to be created shall be uniformly spelled and pronounced in all countries. We now come to the question of meaning. (4) Notions might be named with synonymous words in ethnic languages and the technical term in each ethnic language will have to be one of 'agreed convention' [F *couplage de circuits*, E *connections of circuits;* covering the term of gasoline, E *gasoline*, F *essence*, D *Benzin;* E *petrol*, F *essence moteur*, D *Motorenbenzin*]. (5) A class of words which look similar, are pronounced in a similar manner but have evolved a divergent meaning. To determine an agreed convention of meaning a definition would be required. [F *ignorer* = to be ignorant of, not to know, but E *ignore* = F affecter d'ignorer; E *actual* = effectif, réel, véritable, but F *actuel* = E present, of-the-day (Clifton et Laughlin, *Nouveau Dictionnaire*).]

If we study more closely many words already in international use we find that they consist of two parts, the root and the affix [*oper/ate, oper/ation, oper/ator*]. These affixes [*-ate, -ation, -ator*] are used for many words in many European languages. A second kind of affix used [*-ide*] is called a technical suffix; it is used internationally for chemistry and has a definite function. For the purposes of chemical nomenclature it has one meaning only.

XIV—3. *A short survey of scientific nomenclatures*

Darmesteter traces the origin of indirect word derivation back to Morveau in 1782. The first international congress for nomenclature in Geneva in 1892 became the basis of an international understanding. In 1900, 70,000 terms were fixed, a number which grew to 250,000 in 1925. This congress did not standardize the terms but created principles of terminology. This system of rules contained an agreement on the meaning of roots and affixes which was further extended in 1930.

Distinctive roots, which were almost exclusively taken from Latin and Greek, were allotted to the chemical elements and their connexions *sulph-* for sulphur, *ethane* for C_2H_6]. Affixes were fixed with a defined meaning [*-ide, -ite, -ate, hypo-, per-, -ane, -ene, -yne*]. The roots of the code may be combined with these affixes and then obtain monosignificant precision.

We can now distinguish between two classes of foreign words of Latin or Greek origin which are internationally used. (1) Roots being combined for their derivation with affixes which have a variety of meaning or a very extended meaning [*-ation, deleg/ation, determin/ation*].(2) Roots being derived with technical affixes of a defined and monosignificant meaning [*-ide*]. In both groups the terms are spelled and pronounced differently in their respective ethnic languages.

In the class of terms which has a uniform spelling but a different pronunciation we again distinguish between terms with general affixes and those with technical affixes. The Latin nomenclature for anatomy was accepted in 1895 at a congress in Basle. The commission for pharmaceutical nomenclature formed a committee in 1922 which gave a report of the terms used in 16 countries (*Rapport de la*

Commission de la Nomenclature Pharmaceutique, Haag, 1923), and it was found that up to ten different names were used for certain notions, although they were all derived from Latin. One example may illustrate these differences:

Alcool absolutus	in France and England
Spiritus absolutus	in Hungary and Italy
Alcohol absolutus	in Austria, Belgium, Denmark, Finland, Germany, Switzerland, Hungary, Holland, Norway, and Sweden
Alcohol absolutum	in Great Britain and Spain
Alcohol anhydrum	in Spain
Alcohol dehydratum	in the U.S.A.
Spiritus alcoholisatus	in Switzerland.

Different terms were used even in one country owing to the fact that different dictionaries were in use.

Far more complicated were the nomenclatures for zoology and botany. The rules for botany alone form a whole book (John Briquet, *Règles Internationales de la Nomenclature Botanique*, 1912). The many books on this subject illustrate well its difficult nature and the necessity for a fundamental and uniform solution. They show in what ways the authors have attempted a solution before a complete and workable planned auxiliary language was known. Jean Laurent suggested, in 1935, a solution as part of the subject through the planned language Ido in his book *La Langue Internationale Ido et son application aux sciences pharmacologiques*, while E. Wüster discusses the subject at length in the preface to his *Enciklopedia Vortaro*.

XIV—4. Naturalistic and autonomistic principles

The principles of naturalistic and autonomistic auxiliary language patterns divide two schools of thought. Two demands are made upon the code, (1) the terms used shall be similar to those already in existence in the ethnic languages. They shall be *natural*. Their natural aspect shall be a help in understanding them and in memorizing them. They shall represent the selected material from the Indo-European languages. (2) The roots and affixes shall be easy to compose and their meaning shall be the logical result of their elements. They shall be *regular* and *autonomous*. The composite words shall be formed according to a set of rules easily learned, easily remembered, and easily applied. The knowledge of these rules shall make it possible to form new terms from autonomous word-building elements, or to analyse new terms.

These two demands are often contradictory in practice. In the various existing planned language systems, the differences are of degree rather than of principle. Both schools recognize the fundamental validity of these demands but give priority to either the one or the other. For the purposes of interlinguistic discussion they have been termed the naturalistic school and the autonomistic school. (Professor Debrunner suggested as an alternative term 'highly systematic' for the latter.) As has already been made clear, the autonomistic school comprises Esperanto and Ido, the naturalistic school comprises Latino sine flexione and Occidental, while Novial contains traits common to both. Where the comparisons are made between Ido and Occidental, the argument generally applies equally to the other languages of one of the two schools.

The code for technology shall be nothing else than an international system of fixed terms. The fundamental demands made upon it are, (1) that it shall be able to absorb the hitherto used international systems consisting of language material (in contrast to decimal classification), (2) that it shall be so formed that it is able, within its own system of rules, to extend to new scientific discoveries and spheres, and (3) that it shall be uniform in writing, pronunciation, and meaning in all countries.

The naturalistic and autonomistic schools draw different conclusions from the linguistic material of the ethnic languages and the experiences of earlier systems of planned languages. The main differences can be classified under four headings, (1) spelling, (2) classifying or determinative word endings [-i, -ar, -as, -is, -os, -o, oj, etc.], (3) word derivation, (4) selection of roots. Wüster treats these four problems in the sequence of their relative importance for the code. Word derivation is the main problem, followed by indicative endings, selection of word elements (roots and affixes), and spelling.

XIV—5. Word derivation and the code

In a word like *standard/ization*, *standard-* represents the root, *-ization* the derivative element, termed the affix. If the affix precedes the root [*dis/favour*] it is termed the prefix; if it follows the root [*standard/ize*] it is termed the suffix.

Do the ethnic languages provide all elements for the code, and could these elements form the code without conforming to a uniform pattern? An example might clarify this demand:

English	French	German
calibr/at/ion	tar/age, étalonn/age	Eich/ung
calibr/at/ed	tar/é, étalonn/é	ge/eich/t
standard/iz/ed	normal/is/é	ge/norm/t

If the extent to which a language is spoken were a criterion for accepting its terms into the code without modification, the result would be a terminology consisting of a mixture of the derivatives of the European languages. It would be more difficult to learn than a complete language if we consider that the final code might have to contain several million terms.

In a uniform code we cannot admit different verbal endings [-ed, -é, -t] only because we may accept the root from either English, French, or German. For the sake of facility and precision the affixes will have to be autonomously designed for their purposes. Can we use affixes already internationally known, and will they have to be modified or defined in their meaning?

No serious objections have been raised by those interested in the code against the necessity of a system of affixes. The differences of opinion relate to the question of whether each affix should have one well-defined meaning, or whether several affixes may stand for one meaning [*consider/ation, persist/ence*], or whether affixes may have extended meanings, *i.e.*, one affix covering a variety of root modifications. It may be questioned whether in some cases the verbal noun should end in *-at/ion* and in some cases in *-age*. The comparisons in the following tables are mainly in Ido and Occidental. Ido represents the most highly autonomistic system while Occidental is the chief system representing the naturalistic school.

1	*Ido*	am/ar	esper/ar	pas/ar	promen/ar	penetr/ar
	Occ.	ama/r	espera/r	passa/r	promena/r	penetra/r
2	*Ido*	am/o, amor/o★	esper/o	pas/o	promen/o	penetr/o
	Occ.	am/ore	espera/n/tie, *also* espera	pass/age	promena/da	penetra/t/ion
3	*Ido*	uz/ar	sent/ar	dorm/ar	bruis/ar	efik/ar	infekt/ar
	Occ.	usa/r	senti/r	dormi/r	brui/r	effecte/r	infecte/r
4	*Ido*	uz/o	sent/o	dorm/o	bruis/o	efik/o, efekt/o★	infekt/o
	Occ.	usa, usu, *or* usa/t/ion	senti/ment	dormi/e	brui	effect	infect/ion

★ New roots.

The lines one and three show the infinitive forms of the verbs, while two and four show the nouns.

Ido forms the noun *am/o* = love from *am/ar* = to love. It also has a separate root *amor-*. Occidental forms the noun *am/ore* from *ama/r*. While Ido never modifies the root, Occidental suppresses the final root vowel [*a*] to add the affix *-ore*.

The roots of both languages differ only slightly. The main difference is in the use of the affixes. Ido derives the verbal noun by adding *-o* to the root. This verbal noun, without a qualifying affix, expresses always the action or state [*skrib/ar* = to write, *skrib/o* = writing; *labor/ar* = to work, *labor/o* = working; *telefon/ar* = to telephone, *telefon/o* = the action of telephoning as against *telefon/il/o* = telephone, the instrument]. For the purpose of maintaining the international aspect of the word, Occidental uses many different endings for the verbal noun [*-ore, -nt/ie, -age, -da, -ion, -ment, -e*]. This enables Occidental to retain in its vocabulary most of the known forms of the ethnic languages, while Esperanto and Ido are more rigid in their strict application of their rules of derivation. The question of the exact meaning of the various affixes both in the naturalistic and autonomistic systems is fully discussed elsewhere.

A further comparison between verbal infinitives and verbal nouns of Ido and Occidental shows that the verbal root in Ido generally ends with a consonant while in Occidental it ends either in *-a*, *-i*, or

-e and is sometimes suppressed in its derivatives. The following table makes this clear:

Ido	..	penetr/ar	fin/ar	flex/ar
Occ.	..	penetra/r	fini/r	flexe/r
Ido	..	penetr/o	fin/o	flex/o (flexion/o)*
Occ.	..	penetra/t/ion	fini/t/ion	flex/ion
Ido	..	esper/ar	experienc/ar	difer/ar
Occ.	..	espera/r	experi/r	differe/r
Ido	..	esper/o	experienc/o	difer/o
Occ.	..	espera/nt/ie	experi/ent/ie	differe/nt/ie

In Occidental the final vowel of the root has to be memorized. Occidental follows the conjugation of the Romanic languages. Its advantage is that it maintains a greater similarity to the ethnic languages in their derived forms.

In Ido both root and affix are unchangeable in form and meaning. In Occidental these elements are variable and depend on the final root vowel [-ntie after espera and differe, but -entie after experi]. The rule itself says, 'If the removal of the -(e)r leaves a vowel, add t, or change y into t [crea/r, crea/t/ion, crea/t/iv, crea/t/or; atiny-e/r, atin/t/ion]. If the removal of (e)r leaves either of the consonants d or r, change this letter into s [decide/r, deci-s/ion; adher-e/r, adhe-s/ion]. There are some exceptions to this rule which is more fully discussed in Chapter III, under rules of derivation. The verbal root ending -e is suppressed so that the international word form can be regularly derived [flexe/r, flex/ion]. Owing to its autonomistic structure, Ido can not follow that pattern [flex/ar = to bend, flex/o = the action of bending]. To obtain the meaning for the grammatical term flexion, Ido had to adopt a new root [flexion/o].

A comparative table of root changes in Occidental with the unchangeable forms of Ido explains this point more fully.

Ido	disting/ar	entrapren/ar	vid/ar	kur/ar
Occ.	distinye/r	inter/prende/r	vide/r	curre/r
Ido	disting/o	entrapren/o	vid/o	kur/o
Occ.	distin/t/ion	inter/pren/s/e	vide, vi/s/ion	cur/s
Ido	ced/ar	ad/ven/ar	reten/ar	
Occ.	cede/r	ad/veni/r	re/tene/r	
Ido	ced/o	ad/ven/o	reten/o	
Occ.	ce/ss/ion	ad/ven/t, ad/ven/t/ion	re/ten/t/ion	

If we apply de Wahl's rule to the derivation of Occidental, we can still say that this derivation is regular with few exceptions [cede/r, ce/ss/ion].

XIV—6. Indirect derivation

Where Occidental and Ido use modifying affixes as in indirect or mediate derivation, the differences of principle of the two schools become more apparent.

Ido	eduk/ar		protekt/ar
Occ.	educa/r		protecte/r
Ido	eduk/o	eduk/ist/o	protekt/o, -/ant/o, -ist/o
Occ.	educa/t/ion	educa/t/or	protect/ion, -or
Ido	eduk/al/a	eduk/ist/o	protekt/em/ist/o
Occ.	educa/t/ion/al	educa/t/ion/al/ist	protect/ion/ist

To appreciate the shades of meaning, the respective lists of affixes in Chapters II and III ought to be studied. The table shows that because of its autonomistic regularity of all elements, Ido does not maintain the international aspect of the word in its derived form, while Occidental does maintain the international aspect by applying a more involved set of rules, by lesser precision of its affixes, and by admitting certain irregularities [*protecte/r, protect/or*].

Occidental derives these words from an assumed common root but the original meaning of the root is no longer apparent in all its derived forms [*a-gress-ion, pro-gress, con-gress* (*Cosmoglotta*, XV, 4).]. Many words, whether they are regularly derived as in Occidental, or are accepted as new roots into the vocabulary, will have to be learnt as complete new words. We cannot expect a person unfamiliar with the new language to derive *agression, progress*, and *congress* from a common root. The equivalent Ido terms are *atako, progreso, kongreso.*

Ido	genit/ar, *gener/ar	generator/o	generacion/o	genit/iv/a
Occ.	genera/r	genera/t/or	genera/t/ion	genera/t/iv
E	to generate	generator	generation	generative

The above table shows the Occidental derivation of internationally known words from a common etymological root. The equivalent terms in English and Ido are given. The terms in Ido [*generator/o, generacion/o*] and the affixes [*-or, -t/ion*] are not regularly derived from a root which has lost its common meaning but are accepted as new compound roots into the vocabulary.

A person unfamiliar with the new language will learn *congress, generation, progress* as separate words with one definite meaning, irrespective of whether or not it has been derived from *-gress*, or *genera-*, so that we can say that both schools achieve the same international vocabulary by different means.

XIV—7. *Agglutination and flexion*

The whole system of derivation of both interlinguistic schools can be summed up in two descriptive terms; the derivation of the autonomistic school is agglutinative, the derivation of the naturalistic school is flexional. Agglutination means that roots and suffixes have and maintain (1) one unalterable form, and (2) one unalterable meaning in composition. No new letters are inserted between root and affix in derivation. The flexional derivation does not maintain these principles but regulates them through a set of rules.

The final code shall represent a synthesis of all existing international terminologies, which shall also be able to extend to new fields of scientific activity. We shall therefore examine the existing terminologies as to whether they follow the agglutinative or flexional pattern, and we shall have to examine this question separately for the two main characteristics of agglutination and flexion, (1) the question of monosignificance of the elements in composition and whether

* Precedes a word which has not been officially accepted by the Ido Academy.

affixes are or are not interchangeable, and (2) the question of the flexion of the root and the use of special letters [-*t*, -*s*, etc.].

The principle of monosignificance of the affix is adhered to only if the derived term is a technical one in the existing terminologies. Zoological families and botanical groups end in -*idæ* and -*aceæ*, in medical language inflammations end in -*itis*.

Terms which are common to several sciences and to our daily languages have no fixed scientific meaning for their affixes.

| to isolate | to insulate | to interfere | to resonate |
| isolation | insulation | interference | resonance |

The suffix -*or* is used to indicate the verbal noun with the meaning of acting agent of:

to transform	to insulate	to commutate	to divide	to multiply
transformer	insulator	commutator	divisor	multiplier
transformator				

Alternative suffixes [-*er*, -*nt*, -*iv*] are in use with the same meaning [E *exponent, corrective, nominative;* F *agent;* D *Konzentrant*].

Chemistry is the one science which follows the principle of agglutination (invariability of the root, and monosignificance of the affix) [D *ethane, ethene, ethyne, propane, propene, propyne, butane, butene, butyne*]. Other sciences inflect the root although they may use a monosignificant suffix [*falc/o, falc/on/idæ; appendix, appendi/c/itis, indu/zieren, Indu/kt/anz; divid/e, divi/s/ion, divi/s/or*].

Two questions must be answered for the compilation of the code, (1) should the principle of monosignificance of the affix be accepted? If so we would obtain greater precision of the terms, but would have to give up, in many cases, the international aspect and historical spelling of the new terms, and (2) may a derivation be admitted which permits of the inflexion of the root? If so, we could admit terms already internationally known with little or no modification with the help of a comparatively small number of rules.

These problems are closely interrelated. The admission of affixes with extended meaning is only useful if root inflexion is admitted. Only this double licence would make the introduction of international terms possible. To admit of no root inflexion but extended meaning of affixes would not help us to obtain the international term [*multiplik/ion, divid/ion*].

Only if the inflexion of the root is admitted, together with the extended meaning of the affix, could the international term be formed [*multiplica/t/ion, divi/s/ion*].

Wüster observes that for the purpose of the code a change of the roots might not be necessary, because the code term might already be the inflected root [*multiplication, division*]. Before we can accept this suggestion we must decide whether a code of terms is sufficient, or whether the code will have to consist of a full terminology plus a grammatical system. Only then are we able to define, if necessary, all its terms.

For the verbal roots of the code we find that some do require inflexion while others, in composition with certain affixes, do not [*organisa/r, organisa/t/or; concurre/r, concurre/nt; discusse/r, discuss/ion; producte/r, product/ion*].

De Wahl, the author of Occidental, has been able to formulate a small number of rules for derivation [if the infinitive ending -*r* and the letter -*e*- are removed, thus leaving a vowel, add -*t*-, or change -*y*- into -*t*-; if the removal of -(*e*)*r* leaves either of the two consonants -*d*- or -*r*-, change into -*s*]. De Wahl claims that there are only six exceptions to this rule.

It now remains to be seen whether it is simpler to learn and to apply these rules for the code and thus to obtain the internationally known forms, or to renounce these known forms and retain the exact meaning of both elements (roots and affixes) in their connexions. If de Wahl's suggestion, the flexional derivation, is accepted we will have to consider the addition of definitions for many terms, because we have seen that the elements in flexional connections are not always precise.

The naturalistic school favours flexion and accepts as inevitable the extended meaning of the affixes.

The autonomistic school favours the monosignificance of both roots and affixes, and the invariability of all roots.

XIV—8. *The arguments of both schools*

Scientific studies of comparative ease of learning of autonomistic and naturalistic systems have not yet been undertaken and the opinions generally given are not based on established data by either side, though they are of value for a general appreciation of the problems involved.

The autonomists believe that the non-Romanic peoples have a disadvantage because most roots are taken from Latin and the Romanic languages, for reasons of internationality. Therefore, they argue, non-Romanic people should have the advantage that the connexions of word-elements should be logical and precise, and should not depend on the practices of Romanic languages. The code words formed according to naturalistic principles may be more easily understood by those unfamiliar with the system of derivation, but they may be more difficult to apply with precision in practical use. They also say that a far higher degree of precision can be obtained by autonomistic principles (the principle of reversibility) in new fields of scientific developments where common expressions are not yet known (technology). We cannot, they say, assume that scientists and technicians will always be able to devote a great deal of study to languages, as is still the common practice and necessity today.

The naturalistic school contests these arguments. A great part of the complete derivatives (noun forms) are already known in European languages through international words. The educational value of a naturalistic system, they say, is greater because it affords a rational introduction into the existing international terminologies and the Romanic languages.

It is likely that many people will use the code without learning the fundamental system of derivation. The fact that the code will be comprehensible at first sight would be of greater value than a complete planned language. But we should not lose sight of the possibility that it might have to develop into a complete language so that we shall not be able to add definitions for new terms and processes.

Wüster, in his presentation of the problems, made the very valuable suggestion that the decision between the two principles should not be made hastily on theoretical grounds. It is necessary, he says, that the persons who take the decision should study profoundly the application of both principles. It would be essential that these persons should acquire a thorough knowledge of both. For others who are unable to undertake the necessary studies, the experts should compile extensive comparative lists. These lists would demonstrate how the principles work in practice. The best systems for such a study would be Ido, representing the highly systematic principles (rule of reversibility) of the autonomistic school, and Occidental representing the nearest approach to ethnic languages (de Wahl's rule of derivation) for the naturalistic school. It would also be of advantage to examine Novial (by Otto Jespersen) which is midway between the two, with a leaning towards naturalistic development.

XIV—9. *Indicative endings*

The previous examination has shown that ethnic derivatives cannot be accepted into the code without modification [E *calibr/at/ed* F *tar/é*, D *ge/norm/t*]. They must conform to uniform rules of derivation, in the same way as ethnic derivatives already conform to rules of derivation in their respective nomenclatures. How can we solve this problem?

There is unanimity that the root common to several ethnic languages should be taken with as little modification as possible. The autonomistic languages agree that determinative grammatical endings should show the grammatical character of the word. The naturalistic systems employ this principle only partly. Occidental designates certain adjectives [-*i*], and certain nouns [-*e*, -*a*, -*o*, or -*u*] and nouns in plural [-*s*]. Ido designates all adjectives [-*a*], all nouns in singular [-*o*], in plural [-*i*], and adverbs [-*e*].

If roots are taken from ethnic languages [*fit, differential, collective*] they might be either verbal or substantival roots. For the purpose of the code one of the two should be the principal one, and the second be distinguished by an indicative ending to facilitate its recognition. If we accept the adjectival meaning as the principal one and use the endings of Occidental, we would obtain the forms *differential* and *differentiale, collectiv* and *collective*. If these endings are only used for differentiation, *i.e.*, non-obligatory, Wüster calls them non-pleonastic. They fulfil a similar function as affixes.

Some planned languages, particularly Esperanto and Ido, add a distinctive ending to most roots, indicating to which word-class they belong. The ending for every noun [-o] is obligatory. Wüster calls all obligatory endings pleonastic. The terms applied in this manner are, in my opinion, misleading, as I have tried to make clear in another chapter.

Several reasons are given for pleonastic endings, (1) that it is easier to recognize the meaning of a word if we know, from its ending, to which word-class it belongs. The naturalistic school replies that everybody who understands the roots [*pulvr-*, *grand-*] knows that the first is a noun and the second an adjective. This also applies to derivatives. Those who know the meaning of suffixes also know to which word class they belong. Words ending in -*al* and -*iv* are always adjectives, words ending in -*or* and -*ist* are always nouns, and the noun can always be recognized by adding the definite or indefinite article. This last argument is not convincing because for a code, arranged in the form of a vocabulary, this would be an unnecessary burden; (2) the euphony and ease of pronunciation are increased, particularly if a new ending has to be added to the pleonastic ending [Esperanto -*n* for the accusative, -*j* for plural forms]. The naturalistic school replies: The great languages, English, French, German, do not add an indicative ending to the root. The pleonastic noun-ending should only be added if the root ends in a consonant and a second grammatical consonant has to be added [Occidental *hom-*, *hom/e/s* for the plural]. Ido substitutes -*i* as plural noun-ending, the -*o* being the singular noun ending, and adds the accusative -*n* only in inversion. The reason (2) for Ido remains therefore one of euphony; (3) by adding the pleonastic ending, the code word is definitely classified as such, in contrast to the English, French, and German terms. The same purpose could be obtained by adding a mark of classification to the code word [ISA] as the originator of the code; (4) the pleonastic ending would make it unlikely that the code words are taken over as foreign words into English, French, or German. The same object is reached through the Latin endings for zoological and botanical nomenclatures.

A number of ethnic words complicate the use of pleonastic endings for those words which end in a vowel and where this vowel is an important element determining the sense of the word.

E	hand	manna	door	post	port	post (mail)
Occ.	manu	manna	porta	posto	porto	posta
Ido	manu/o	mana/o	pord/o	posten/o	portu/o	post/o
Esp.	man/o	mana/o	pord/o	posten/o	haven/o	posto/

	E	humanism	humanity			
	Occ.	hom/an/ità	hom/an/itè			
	Ido	human/es/o	hom/ar/o			
	Esp.	human/ec/o	hom/ar/o			

In those cases, to determine the sense of the word, Ido had to change the root slightly [*hom/o*, *homar/o*, *human/es/o; portu/o*]. The zoological term for 'man' is *homo*, which justifies both roots [*hom-*, *human-*].

XIV—10. Spelling

It is assumed that agreement exists amongst all about two principles, (1) that the word-elements should be taken from the ethnic languages preferably unchanged, and (2) that the code-words shall be spelled and pronounced in the same manner in all countries. The many questions arising out of the controversy of phonetic or historic spelling are studied in detail elsewhere, and are consequently not repeated here. They are however of vital importance to the code.

Dr Wüster formulates five questions as the immediate problems of the code, (1) shall the derivation of the code be agglutinative or flexional? (2) shall pleonastic endings be added to the words, or not? (3) shall the spelling be phonetic or historical? (4) shall double consonants be admitted, or not? (5) shall the letters and combinations of letters qu, w, x, y, ph, th, be admitted, or not?

XIV—11. Description and definition

As technology advances new names are required for tools or parts which have not been known before and for which no internationally known terms exist. Principles should be established with which new names can be given according to uniform rules. A variety of deciding factors is practised today, (1) by describing the function of the part [*ejector blade*], by describing the position of the part in the machine [*first* and *second elevator; upper* or *lower air screw*], (3) by describing the aspect of the part [*vice jaws; elevator arm*], (4) by using for the part a name with a qualifying attribute [*bronze spring*]. It is often necessary to add a description or definition to the new name.

In electro-technics every term is followed by its definition [*excitation*: Production of magnetic flux through a magnetic circuit by means of an electric current; the term is sometimes used as a synonym for the magnetomotive force producing the flux through an electro-magnet. (05-30-065, *International Electro-technical Vocabulary*)]. According to the report on the ISA conference on terminology (Paris 1937), Helleboid said that 'the question is, whether in any case a word can be immediately comprehensible. In science and technology it is never certain that a word can be understood immediately. A definition will always be necessary. The majority of scientific terms are compounds and their connexion is not always clear. It will be essential to have a definition for technical and scientific terms because the term must be represented by a word or compound.'

It is now generally agreed that for the purpose of a scientific terminology a definition for each term is desirable, except for such words where no doubt at all is possible. The definitions of technical terms differ sometimes slightly and sometimes considerably in ethnic languages. Usage has often led to word-forms which do not represent their full meaning. Examples of terms and their definition is taken from the *International Electrotechnical Vocabulary* to illustrate what exactly is meant by scientific definition:

(Term 05-25-215)

French

Champ coercitif: Champ magnétique nécessaire pour ramener à une valeur nulle l'aimantation d'un corps ferromagnétique, après qu'on l'a soumis à un nombre de cycles suffisant pour atteindre la stabilité.

English

Coercive force: Magnetic force necessary to bring the magnetization of a ferro-magnetic body to zero, after it has been submitted to a sufficient number of cycles to attain stability.

(Term 05-20-030)

French

Courant électrique : Mouvement d'électricité dans un milieu ou le long d'un circuit. Parfois employé comme abréviation d'intensité de courant. Sauf indication contraire on admet comme sens du courant le sens opposé à celui du mouvement de l'électricité négative.

English

Electric current : Movement of electricity in a medium or along a circuit. Sometimes used as an abbreviation for intensity of current. Unless the contrary is stated, the direction of the current is opposite to that of motion of negative electricity.

(Term 05-40-170)

French

Coefficient de température : 1. Entre deux températures déterminées: (coefficient moyen) quotient de la variation de la propriété considérée par l'écart de température qui la produit.
2. À une température donnée : valeur limite du coefficient moyen lorsque l'écart de température tend vers zéro.

English

Temperature coefficient : 1. Between two given temperatures : (mean coefficient) the quotient of the variation of the property considered, by the difference in temperature producing it.
2. At a given temperature : the limiting value of the mean coefficient when the difference in temperature is very small.

(Term 05-05-005)

French

Grandeurs scalaires : Grandeurs qui peuvent être complètement caractérisées par un seul paramètre, c'est-à-dire par leur valeur numérique rapportée à l'unité de mesure correspondante.

English

Scalar quantities : Quantities which can be completely represented by a single parameter, that is to say, by their numerical value, expressed in terms of the corresponding unit of measurement.

XIV—12. Comparative tables

These tables show clearly some existing difficulties in international terminology, particularly in the gradings of oil (ISA 28, a-b10). The planned language systems consulted for the purpose of these tables were Esperanto, Ido, Occidental, Latino sine flexione.

The members of the ISA-37 Committee (Terminology) decided at their conference in Paris, 1937, to collaborate with the International Auxiliary Language Association (IALA) which has a staff of linguistic workers and is examining the more important planned language systems. The two bodies decided to exchange experiences with each other, without committing themselves to adopt necessarily their respective findings and conclusions.

TABLE II

The terms here given represent an experiment with planned languages to represent their degree of efficiency and precision without giving a definition for the terms. (Compiled by ISA).

Language Group	Dewey Decimal Classification	Language	Term	Term	Term
Germanic-Romanic (170 million)	—2	English	class of fit (... fit)	grade of fit	fit
Romanic (200 million)	—4	French	cas d'ajustement, genre d'ajustement (ajustage à...)	qualité (qualité...)	ajustement
Germanic (90 million)	—3	German	Sitz (... sitz)	Gütegrad (... passung)	Passung (... sitz)
Planned International Languages	—408.92	Esperanto	strikteco de fito, fito, ludo-klaso	kvalito de fito, toleranco-klaso	fito
	—408.942.1	Ido	klaso di fito; *defino:* 'fitar' tale adjustigar mashinala peci, ke oli ne plus movas en irga direciono exter la axala.	grado di fito, qualesala grado di fito	fito
	—	Occidental	casu	qualità	adjustament
	—408.993.232	Latino sine flexione (Interlingua)	adjustament	qualitat	qualitat

XV. The Work of the International Auxiliary Language Association

XV—1. History

THE INTERNATIONAL AUXILIARY LANGUAGE ASSOCIATION (IALA) was founded in 1924 at the instance of the Committee on International Language of the International Research Council. In 1919 the International Research Council, to investigate the problem of a planned language, formed a special committee of which Frederick G. Cottrell, a scientist of wide repute, became chairman. In response to his invitation the American, British, French, and Italian Associations for the Advancement of Science, the American Council of Education, the American Classical League, the American Philological Association, and the National Research Council of the United States formed co-operating committees. This activity led to the formation of IALA which had as its programme the establishment, upon scientific foundations, of an international auxiliary language.

The outstanding personality of IALA was then, and is now, its Honorary Secretary, Mrs Dave Hennen Morris, who has made tireless efforts to further the work undertaken by IALA and its various committees in America and Europe. IALA has sponsored a number of experiments and studies on various aspects of the language problem and mainly on questions which had hitherto been assumed without convincing proof. IALA has had the active assistance of the Research Corporation, which has contributed an annual grant for its activities.

From the beginning IALA has held the conviction that no one of the great national languages will be permanently acceptable as the international auxiliary language. The chief reasons for this view are fully explained in IALA's *Plan* (1936): 'National associations bound up with the major languages; the time and effort entailed in learning a foreign language, not to say several; the constant and sometimes serious misunderstandings that arise in translating one ethnic language into another; the inevitable mutilation of a cultural tongue when adapted to international service (for example Pidgin English). Such desirable qualities as neutrality, grammatical simplicity, and regularity with consequent ease of learning, and maximum freedom from idiom and ambiguity (to be termed, according to Harold E.

Palmer, *irregular collocations*) are to be obtained only in a language deliberately constructed for international use.'

IALA's programme had two main objects in view, (1) to obtain agreement on one definite planned language system and to obtain official sanction for that language, and (2) to secure the general acceptance of the sanctioned language which would include its teaching in the schools. To achieve agreement on a definite system, IALA has established and is maintaining constant touch with representatives of the main auxiliary language systems. The preliminary enquiries sponsored by IALA were (1) investigations in the field of language learning, (2) a survey of the language problems and practices of international conferences, and (3) linguistic studies.

Some of the many meetings and conferences convened by IALA were of particular interest. In 1930 (March 20 to April 2) IALA organized the meeting of linguistic research in Geneva, presided over by Professor Otto Jespersen. This was the first meeting of its kind where linguists and interlinguists were brought together to discuss the main problems of a planned language. Prominent philologists met there with representatives of Esperanto, Ido, Nov-Esperanto, Occidental, and Latino sine flexione. Its direct result was that the congress of linguists, which took place a year later in the same town, expressed its appreciation of the work of IALA for an auxiliary language, and gave a general promise that scientists would contribute their share towards an evolution which is necessary and which will some day attain its goal. The latter congress was presided over by Professor Meillet whose interest in an auxiliary language and in Ido in particular is well known; as early as 1918 he pleaded the case of a constructed language in his *Les Langues dans l'Europe Nouvelle* (Payot, Paris).

The meeting of linguists at Copenhagen (August 1936), organized by IALA, attracted great attention in the linguistic world. Shortly before it took place IALA formulated its *Plan for obtaining agreement on an auxiliary world-language* which contained a detailed description of the task envisaged by IALA, the linguistic research to be undertaken and promoted, a mention of the project of an International Language Academy which is to maintain the stability and guide the development of the language, and the policy of IALA.

At this conference Professor Collinson (University of Liverpool), one of the linguistic collaborators on IALA's staff, mentioned that IALA had decided to admit as candidate languages the systems *Esperanto, Esperanto-II, Ido, Novial, Occidental,* and *Latino sine flexione (Interlingua).* These languages are referred to by IALA as 'existing, constructed languages of demonstrated usefulness.' A definition of this reference is given by IALA (Committee for Agreement, July 1936), (1) the language must be one that is already well developed, with vocabulary, grammar, and system of word formation, and not a mere project, and (2) the language must be in use as a means of communication both in speech and writing, adequate for all ordinary purposes. In regard to the written language there must exist publications sufficient to prove such adequacy. IALA has made clear its policy to build upon the fund of experience and knowledge furnished by the languages which have been tested by time and use. For a number of years it explored the possibility of selecting one of the above mentioned 'candidate languages' as a base-language from which a definitive form of language might be developed (*see* p.147).

XV—2. Experiments and research

Over the last twenty-two years IALA sponsored many enquiries of a technical and general character; these have been reported in books, annual reports, and language monographs and are briefly summarized here.

Professor Thorndike (Columbia University) has conducted, on behalf of IALA, a six-year experimental course to determine the relative ease of learning a constructed language as compared with learning an ethnic language, and to determine the influence of the study of a constructed language on subsequent language learning, both in the vernacular and foreign languages. Thorndike said that 'on the whole, with expenditures of from ten to a hundred hours, the achievement in the synthetic language will probably be from five to fifteen times that in a natural language, according to the difficulty of the latter.' (p. 7, *Language Learning*, 1933, Columbia University). A brief review of this work appeared in IALA's *Annual Report*, 1939. In a senior high school in the U.S. a group of pupils studied IALA's general language course which used Esperanto as a medium to show the relationship in words and in word-building between English, French, Spanish, Latin, and German. Another class studied French in the usual manner of the school as the first foreign language. Both groups studied five times a week for 45-minute periods. The result was that the average gain made by the students of the general language course in English vocabulary was 6.68 as against the 3.75 of the group studying French as the only foreign language.

Another experiment which brings out more clearly the advantages to be derived from the preliminary study of a planned language as a general introduction to language learning is provided by the results obtained at a junior high school. One group studied the general language course during one term twice a week for 45-minute periods on a voluntary basis. For the following term they joined other pupils in a beginners' class in Latin. An initial test, taken before the term began, showed that the language course pupils made 7 points against the 5 points of the other pupils. At the end of the term a second test was made in which the former language course pupils obtained 14.5 points against 12.4 of the other pupils. The final results averaged 21.5 for the former language course pupils and 17.4 for the others.

The conclusion reached was that the preliminary study of a Latin-derived constructed language as a kind of language model simplifies and clarifies for the pupils the problems encountered in language learning, that it has definite advantages for the study of foreign languages, and that it aids the comprehension of English words. The course used in these experiments was that compiled by Helen S. Eaton, the linguistic research associate of IALA.

The late Herbert N. Shenton, Professor of Sociology of Syracuse University, completed for IALA in 1933 a pioneer study of non-governmental, internacional organizations as a four-fold inquiry :

What do people desire to talk about?
Where do they assemble for conference?
What nationalities participate?
How do people of diverse mother tongues manage to converse?

Professor Shenton's study was published as *Cosmopolitan Conversation, the Language Problems of International Conferences*, Columbia University Press.

The international conference movement was outlined from its beginnings. In 1840–49 there was an average of only one conference a year. In the decade following World War I private international organizations with their periodic conferences formed a world-wide network of international cooperation in practically every field of human affairs.

By means of a questionnaire and correspondence, Professor Shenton obtained data from 607 organizations concerning their conferences. These data revealed that about 300 international conferences took place every year from 1921 through 1929 bringing together assemblies of different nationals from two or three countries up to more than a score of countries.

Organizations were classified under fourteen types according to their respective subjects of interest: Pacifism; Law and Administration; Labour; Education; Feminism; Sport and Tourism; Humanitarianism, Religion and Morals; Economics and Finance; Agriculture; Trade and Industry; Communications and Transit; Arts and Sciences; Medicine and Hygiene; and Miscellaneous which included the various propagandist organizations for Esperanto, Ido, Occidental, and Latino sine Flexione.

In general, language difficulties were handled by 'Official languages, languages of publication and correspondence, translation languages, permitted languages'. English, French, and German were the languages most frequently recognized, but the trend was to increase the number of languages admitted in conferences.

Significant interest in the use of an auxiliary language was revealed and a special section of the book was devoted to this aspect. The successful congresses held by Esperantists and also by Idists gave proof of the practicability of a constructed language.

Professor Shenton's book remains an historical reference work of great value for the present-day approach to an analytical study of the language problem in international conferences.

World War II disrupted the activities of international organizations but in our present post-war world there is increasing evidence that the social institution of the private international conference is being used by scientists, educators, and welfare groups alongside the governmental committees and commissions of the United Nations. Much publicity has been given to the language difficulties of the United Nations. The San Francisco Charter was published in five official languages. Russian is admitted in the Security Council. Interpretation from French to English and English to French slows down the proceedings of the Assembly. Simultaneous translations are given by telephone at some meetings. The question of a common language to expedite the future work of UNO is receiving more serious public attention than ever before accorded the idea of an auxiliary language.

Another piece of research, of the greatest practical value irrespective of the final form of the auxiliary language, is the compilation of the *Semantic Frequency List* (University of Chicago Press) undertaken in 1934 by Helen S. Eaton of IALA's staff. The list is based on word counts in different languages, *i.e.*, *Teachers' Word Book of 20,000 Words* by Thorndike, *French Word Book* by Vander Beke, *Häufigkeitswörterbuch der deutschen Sprache* by Kaeding, and the *Graded Spanish Word Book* by Buchanan. It shows the relative frequency of approximately 6,000 international concepts with common or related semantic values in four of the great European languages.

The 6,474 concepts are arranged on a scale of descending frequency, as determined by their frequency position in the four individual languages examined: English, French, German, and Spanish. As one language had to be selected for the 'key words' or 'finding words' for the concepts, English was chosen; and the other languages follow in the order given above. This does not mean, however, that the List was made entirely from the English approach. The English source list was examined first, and equivalents for the English words in the other three language lists were sought.

XV—3. Vocabulary selection

IALA's *General Report* 1945, published in July of the same year, includes a brief review of IALA's aims and activities from the foundation of the Association at the end of 1924. The report is mainly devoted to an outline of the methods and results of IALA's linguistic research.

After much experimentation the idea of selecting one of the existing systems of demonstrated usefulness as a base-language has been broadened. It has been found to be more practicable to start from the basis which underlies all six of the 'candidate languages' rather than from any one of them, namely the basis of the international vocabulary, or, in other terms, the words common to the greatest number of widely distributed cultural languages.

The basic procedure for the selection of the vocabulary includes, (1) the setting up of control languages to be referred to as control units; (2) the application of three rules for the choice of international words and the standardization of their forms and meanings in the auxiliary language vocabulary; (3) supplementary devices which assure that the auxiliary language vocabulary includes all words needed for practical purposes. The three rules referred to under (2) have the purpose of determining (a) in how many of the four control units an international word must be found in order to be eligible for representation in the auxiliary language; (b) in what form an eligible word is to be standardized; (c) what meaning or meanings it is to convey.

The four control units for the selection of the vocabulary are English, French, Italian, Spanish and Portuguese, the latter two forming one unit as closely related languages. These units are the basic point of departure, giving IALA's projected system an Anglo-Romanic basis. The three criteria for obtaining standardized international words are as follows:

(1) ELIGIBILITY

'If an international word is represented by variants with at least one common meaning in at least three out of the four control units—English, French, Italian, Spanish-Portuguese—it is eligible for representation in the auxiliary language.'

(2) FORM

'The standardized form in which an eligible international word is represented is a common-denominator form of all its variants and may be called their *prototype*. The prototype is arrived at by a thorough study of the etymology of the word-family in which the international word is found.'

(3) MEANING

'The meaning or meanings of a standardized international word are the meaning or meanings which the variants contributing to its eligibility have in common.'

The supplementary devices necessary for the selection of words which cannot be obtained by the strict application of the above three rules vary in character, though they do not differ in principle from similar procedures as applied in some of the existing systems of constructed languages.

IALA has classified existing systems into two schools already known to the reader, (a) the naturalistic school, and (b) the autonomistic school or, as IALA prefers to call it, the schematic school. The procedure of word selection as described produces words of the naturalistic type. To transform the naturalistic words into words for the autonomistic language model, it is necessary to apply certain additional procedures designed to regularize word-formation, spelling, and pronunciation. Here again various degrees of regularization are possible, and IALA has, so far, developed two models, referred to in the report as *schematic E* in which the regularization is the minimum possible, and *schematic K* which represents the medium degree of regularization. Further regularization is possible, though not without sacrificing international recognizability of the meaning of the text to those familiar with English and one or more of the Romanic languages. In all three models the roots remain the same, though the form of a word may be altered through the use of different suffixes, *e.g.*, the adjectives *severe* and *prompt* are standardized as *severe* and *prompte*. The nouns *severity* and *promptitude* have, in the naturalistic model, the form of *severitate* and *promptitudine*, while schematic E has *severitá* and *promptitá*, and schematic K has *severeso and prompteso*, *-eso* being derived from Latin with its equivalents of *-esse* in French, *-ezza* in Italian, *-eza* in Spanish and Portuguese.

The principles applied for the change from the naturalistic word to either of the schematic models are as follows, (1) all naturalistic words are examined in the framework of the etymological families of which they are part. Each etymological family is divided into what IALA terms *schematic groups*, each group headed by an invariable root. Added to that there are standardized affixes, *i.e.*, prefixes and suffixes and rules for using them; (2) a naturalistic word whose meaning can be expressed by a base word plus one or more of the standardized affixes, is given a form made up of the base word, less its final vowel, and the appropriate standardized affix or affixes; (3) a naturalistic word is not subjected to this schematic treatment when it has a meaning which cannot be expressed by the formation of a schematic word from a root plus one or more of the standardized affixes, but is taken over bodily into the schematic vocabulary after adaptation in spelling.

The actual difference between a naturalistic word and one of the schematic models is the regularization with which the latter is formed and the possibility of combining it with standardized affixes vastly extending its potential range as a root of a semantic group. IALA estimates that the proportion of naturalistic words requiring a different affix in the schematic version is as little as, approximately, ten per cent.

XV—4. Experimental versions in three models

Little is as yet known of the grammar of the three models from the report. The three texts represent the present state of progress of IALA's work. On comparison it will be found that the naturalistic model has much in common both with Interlingua and Occidental, while the schematic K model is not far removed from Ido and Novial in their present form. The final language to be recommended by IALA will not greatly differ from one of the three models represented here, so that we have, today, a fairly clear idea of what that language will be, as confirmed in IALA's words, 'when, as the result of its research, experimentation, and consultation, IALA decides which type of language it will recommend, it will proceed to develop a single model of that type which will not be fundamentally different from the models of that type in this report.'

Naturalistic model

Key to pronunciation: In all versions the stress normally falls on the vowel preceding the last consonant. In naturalistic and schematic E exceptions may be made to conform to the way certain words are stressed in the Romanic languages. In all versions the addition of -s to form the plural does not change the stress.

c   before *e* and *i* = ts, s, or ch in church
c   in other positions = k
g   before *e* and *i* = j, z in azure, or g in go
j   = y in yes, j in joke, or z in azure
qu before *e* and *i* = qu in queen, or like k
qu in other positions = qu in queen
t   in combinations tia, tie, tio = ts, s in sun, or t in top (but always as t in the word *questione*)
t   in other positions = t in table

Le pace, como le libertate, require constante devotione et incessante vigilantia. Ille require le voluntate de prendere mensuras concrete pro su conservatione. Ille require constante cooperatione inter le nationes et le determinatione de vivere in commune como bone vicinos in un mundo de bone vicinos. Le pace require le acceptatione de le idea que su mantenentia es un causa commune sic pretiose et sic immensamente importante que omne differentias et controversias inter le naciones pote et debe essere resolvite per le uso de medios pacific.

(Excerpt from speech of Hon. Cordell Hull, August 21st, 1944.)

Schematic E model

Key to pronunciation:
c   before *e* and *i* = ch in church
c   in other positions = k
g   = g in go, in all positions
j   = j in joke
qu = qu in queen, in all positions
t   = t in top, in all positions
The apostrophe is used to indicate irregular stress

Le pace, como le liberita', require constante devotion et incesante vigilantia. Elo require le volentia de prender mensuras concrete por su conservation. Elo require constante cooperation entre le nationes e le determination de viver ensemble como bon vicinos in un mundo de bon vicinos. Le pace require le acceptation del idea ke su manteno es un causa comun tan pretiose e tan imensemente importante ke omne diferentias e controversias entre le nationes, pote e deve eser resoluete per le uso de medios pacifike.

Schematic K model

Key to pronunciation:
c = ts, in all positions
g = g in go, in all positions
j = j in joke
qu = qu in queen, in all positions
t = t in top, in all positions

Le paco, kom le libereso, require konstante devoto et noncesante vigilantso. Id require le volentso de prendere konkrete mensuros por su konservo. Id require konstante koopero inter le nacionos et le determino de vivere ensemble kom bone vicinos in un mundo de bone vicinos. Le paco require le akcepto del ideo ke su manteno es un komune kauso tan preciose et tan imensemen importante ke omne diferentsos et kontroversios inter le nacionos pote et deve essere resoluete per le uso de pacifike medios.

XV—5. *Consultation*

From the beginning of its activities IALA has kept in touch with leaders in the field of planned languages, with eminent linguists, and with people of experience in international affairs.

In October 1946, IALA issued a technical questionnaire in English and French dealing with many features of its experimental models. This questionnaire was prepared by Professor André Martinet (Paris) and Professor J. P. Vinay (formerly Paris, now Montreal). It contains summaries of the grammatical features of a naturalistic model and two schematic models, a list of all affixes used in the two schematic models, and 127 questions soliciting opinions and suggestions regarding structural details. It has been distributed to representative inter linguists and to certain linguists in a number of countries.

At the time of publication of the present work, IALA is experimenting with additional models of the auxiliary language. All of its models are variants of the emerging interlingua which it will finally recommend. Further samples of experimental models are soon to be published, in a pamphlet also prepared by Professors Martinet and Vinay. The texts will be presented in such a way that they can be easily compared. They will be accompanied by explanatory matter in five languages: English, French, Spanish, German, and Russian. The pamphlet will include about half a dozen questions asking the reader for his reactions to IALA's different models. He needs no special linguistic knowledge in order to answer the questions. The pamphlet will be distributed much more widely than the technical questionnaire, to people of many different fields of interest.

Both the technical questionnaire and the pamphlet of sample texts are aimed to gather opinions that will be valuable to IALA in determining the definitive form of auxiliary language it will recommend.

XV—6. IALA's place in the auxiliary language movement

IALA has established its claim as an impartial and scientific investigator in the field of a constructed auxiliary language. Under the direction of its honorary secretary, Mrs Dave Hennen Morris, IALA has obtained the interest of a gradually increasing number of professional linguists who no longer regard the analysis of languages as they are as their sole task but who have contributed, out of their experience and vast knowledge, to the study of the language problem.

An important factor for the success of IALA's future efforts will be the official support it can secure from authorities in different countries and from scientific, educational, and commercial organizations interested in and concerned with its decisions. The stronger that support, the more definite can be the final form of the language envisaged. The degree of support will decide the likelihood of the immediate application and introduction of the auxiliary language. Should the support be insufficient to secure the introduction of the language proposed, it will have been IALA's contribution to have established, scientifically, the principles which are most likely to ead to the formulation of a common auxiliary language.

Bibliography

Academia pro Interlingua, *Key to and primer of Interlingua*, London 1931 (Kegan Paul)

S. Auerbach, *Pri nonmediati derivatione in li international lingues*, in *Grammatical Miscellany* (Allen & Unwin)

Louis de Beaufront, *Complete manual of the auxiliary language Ido*, London 1919 (Pitman)

de Beaufront-Couturat, *Dictionnaire Français-Ido*, Paris 1915 (Chaix)

Louis de Beaufront, *Kompleta gramatiko detaloza di la linguo internaciona Ido*, Luxembourg 1925 (Meier-Heucké)

Ric Berger, *Li derivation in li lingue international*, in *Cosmoglotta*, Chapelle 1937 (Occidental-Union)

Ric Berger, *Li ver historie del lingue international*, in *Cosmoglotta*, Chapelle 1937 (Occidental-Union)

Ric Berger, *Ortografic decisiones del Francés Academie*, in *Cosmoglotta* XVII, 4, Chapelle 1938 (Occidental-Union)

Dr Frederick Bodmer, *The Loom of Language*, London 1943 (Allen & Unwin)

British Association for the Advancement of Science, *Post-war University Education, interim report*, in *The Advancement of Science*, London 1942

British Association for the Advancement of Science, *Report on an international auxiliary language*, Edinburgh 1921 (British Association)

Montague C. Butler, *Step by Step in Esperanto*, London 1933 (Esperanto-Association)

Gaetano Canesi-L. Weber, *Lectiones de lingua auxiliare internationale Interlingua* (Latino sine flexione), Lwów 1938 (Ekonomia)

William Edward Collinson, *Indication, a study of demonstratives, articles, and other 'Indicators'*, as a Language Monograph, Baltimore 1937 (Waverly Press)

Cosmoglotta, Chapelle 1935-1939 (Occidental-Union)

Cosmoglotta-B, Chapelle 1937-1939 (Occidental-Union)

Louis Couturat, *Studyo pri la derivado*, Paris 1910 (Delagrave)

Couturat-Feder, *Grosses Wörterbuch Deutsch-Ido*, Paris 1920 (Chaix)

Couturat-Jespersen-Lorenz-Ostwald-Pfaundler-Donnan, *International Language and Science*, London 1910 (Constable)

L. Couturat-L. Leau, *Histoire de la langue Universelle*, Paris 1907 (deuxième tirage), first published 1903 (Librairie Hachette)

Louis Couturat-L. Leau, *Les Nouvelles Langues Internationales*, Paris 1907

Délégation pour l'adoption d'une langue internationale, *Conclusions du rapport*, Paris 1907

Johannes Dietterle, *Originala verkaro*, Leipzig 1929

Drezen-Chatelain-Spielrein-Shirkoff, *Ueber einen internationalen terminologischen Code*, Kommission für technische Terminologie der Akademie der Wissenschaften der USSR, November 1935

E. Drezen, *Historio de la Mondlingvo*, Leipzig 1931 (Ekrelo)

E. D. Durrant, *The Language Problem*, London 1943 (Esperanto Publishing Co.)

Luther H. Dyer, *English-Ido Dictionary*, London 1924 (International Language Society)

Luther H. Dyer, *Ido-English Dictionary*, London 1924 (Pitman)

Luther H. Dyer, *The problem of an international auxiliary language and its solution in Ido*, London 1923 (Pitman)

Helen S. Eaton, *Semantic Frequency List*, Chicago 1940 (University Press)

Helen S. Eaton, *The educational value of an artificial language*, in *Modern Language Journal*, New York 1927

Esperanto Pocket Dictionary, The 'Edinburgh', London 1931 (Nelson)

Feder-Schneeberger, *Vollständiges Wurzelwörterbuch Ido-Deutsch*, Lüsslingen 1919 (Ido-Weltsprache-Verlag)

Ilmari Federn, *Li paroles international e li mutation del radicas*, in *Cosmoglotta-B*, Chapelle 1937 (Occidental-Union)

Ilmari Federn, *Occidental-Grundlage für einen internationalen terminologischen Code*, Copenhagen 1936

Ilmari Federn, *Spiritu de Occidental, li ovre de Edgar de Wahl*, Chapelle 1938 (Institute Occidental)

Federn-Kemp-Haislund, *Occidental-English vocabulary*, Chapelle 1937 (Institute Occidental)

F. N. Finck, *Die Haupttypen des Sprachbaus*, Leipzig-Berlin 1923 (Teubner)

J. R. Firth, *Speech*, London 1930 (Ernest Benn)

J. R. Firth, *The Tongues of Men*, London 1937 (Watts & Co.)

H. W. Fowler, *A Dictionary of Modern English Usage*, Oxford 1940 (Clarendon Press)

Sir Richard Gregory, *International standards and systems*, in *Nature*, No. 3813 (Macmillan)

Grosjean-Maupin, Esselin, Grenkamp-Kornfeld, Waringhien, *Plena Vortaro de Esperanto*, dua eldono, Paris 1934 (SAT)

Albert Léon Guérard, *A Short History of the International Language Movement*, London 1922 (T. Fisher Unwin)

L. M. de Guesnet, *L'Occ dental, langue d'intercompréhension immédiate*, Paris 1928 (Occidental-Buro)

J. Guignon, *Lexique-Manuel Ido-Français*, Fontainebleau 1924 (Pouyé)

Hans Homolka, *Grundsätzliches zur Frage des internationalen terminologischen Code*, Wien 1936 (Occidental-Union)

IALA (International Auxiliary Language Association), *Annual Reports*, New York

IALA, *A Plan for obtaining Agreement on an Auxiliary World Language*, New York 1936

IALA, *Communications from Committee for Agreement*, The Hague 1936

IALA, *Comparative Studies of International Languages*, Liverpool 1936

IALA, *Comparative Texts*, 1937

IALA, *Some Criteria for an International Language and Commentary*, Brussels 1936

IALA, *General Report 1945*, New York 1945

Interlinguisticus, *Logica in li lingue auxiliari*, in *Cosmoglotta-B*, Chapelle 1939 (Occidental-Union)

International Electrotechnical Commission, *International Electrotechnical Vocabulary*, London 1935 (I.E.C.)

ISA 37 (International Federation of National Standardizing Associations) Terminologie, *Bericht über die Sitzungen in Paris*, 1937

ISA 37 Terminologie, *Bericht über die Sitzungen in Budapest*, 1936

H. Jacob, *Esperanto-Ido Vortaro*, London 1934 (Ido-Uniono)

H. Jacob, *Otto Jespersen, His Work for an International Auxiliary Language*, London 1943 (Ido-Society)

H. Jacob, *Möglichkeit der Anwendung der Plansprache Ido für den internationalen terminologischen Code*, London 1936 (Ido-Uniono)

H. Jacob, *On the Choice of a Common Language*, London 1946 (Pitman)

J. Hubert Jagger, *English in the Future*, London 1940 (Nelson)

Karl Janotta, *Leitfaden der Weltsprache Occidental*, Stuttgart 1931 (Franckh)

Otto Jespersen, *An International Language*, London 1928 (Allen & Unwin)

Otto Jespersen, *Critikal remarkes al criteries de IALA*, in *Novialiste*, Stockholm 1938 (P. Ahlberg)

Otto Jespersen, *History of Our Language—Artificial Languages after the World War*, London 1920 (Ido-Society)

Otto Jespersen, *Language, Its Nature, Development and Origin*, London 1922 (Allen & Unwin)

Otto Jespersen, *Men labore por un international lingue*, in *Novialiste* 18/19, Stockholm 1937/8 (P. Ahlberg)

Otto Jespersen, *Novial Lexike*, London 1930 (Allen & Unwin)

Otto Jespersen, *Plubonisat Novial*, in *Novialiste*, Stockholm 1934 (P. Ahlberg)

O. Jespersen-E. de Wahl, *Discussion pri international lingue*, in *Novialiste*, Stockholm 1935 (P. Ahlberg)

Jean Laurent, *Jurnalo de farmacio e kemio*, translation of a complete number in Ido, Paris 1933 (XVIII, 4) (Doin & Cie.)

Jean Laurent, *La langue internationale Ido (Esperanto réformé) et son application aux sciences pharmacologiques*, Marseille 1935 (Petit Marseillais)

A. Lavagnini, *Mondi-Linguo, a grammatical outline*, Mexico 1943

Lébasnier, *Dérivation et composition*, Paris 1912 (Imprimerie Chaix)

Karl J. Loy, *Taschenwörterbuch Deutsch-Esperanto*, Berlin-Dresden 1923 (Ellersiek & Borel)

Nicola Mastropaolo, *Schola et Vita*, Milano 1936-1939 (Academia pro Interlingua)

A. Meillet, *Les langues dans l'Europe nouvelle*, Paris 1918 (Payot)

Karl Minor, *Esperanto-Deutsches Handwörterbuch*, Berlin-Dresden 1924 (Ellersiek & Borel)

Albert Noetzli, *Vergleichende Grammatik des Esperanto und Ido*, Zürich (Ido-Verlag)

Nordin-Feder-Roos, *Internaciona radio-lexiko en Ido e Germana, Angla, Franca, Italiana e Hispana kun defini, formuli, tabeli, etc.*, Stockholm 1924 (P. Ahlberg)

Novial, Elementes gramatikali de li lingue international, Stockholm 1933 (P. Ahlberg)

Novialiste, Stockholm 1934-1939 (P. Ahlberg)

Hanns Oertel, *Lectures on the Study of Language*, New York 1909 (Scribner's Sons)

R. A. S. Paget, *A World Language*, in *Nature*, 3820, London 1943 (Macmillan)

Guiseppe Peano, *Interlingua*, Torino 1927 (Academio pro Interlingua)

Marcel Pesch, *Listo de 250 grupi ek Ido-vorti ofte mis-uzata*, ek Progreso, Genève 1930

Marcel Pesch, *Radikaro Ido-Ido*, *Centerbladet*, Oerebro 1935-1939

E. Pigal, *Okzidental, die Weltsprache*, Stuttgart 1931 (Franckh)

Progreso, Paris 1908-1946 (Ido-Uniono)

S. Quarfood, *La Akademio*, Oerebro 1936 (Ido-Editerio)

Question de la langue universelle, la demande adressée à la Société des Nations, Stockholm 1921

A. Z. Ramstedt, *Li psykologie e sociologic caractere del lingues*, in *Cosmoglotta*, IV, 39-40, 1927 (Occidental-Union)

Raxworthy, *Introductory Occidental Grammar*, London (The Britannic Occidental Association)

Janis Roze, *Raporto, decidi dil akademio interimal e du suplementi*, Riga 1937

Stanley Rundle, *Language as a social and political factor in Europe*, London 1946 (Faber & Faber)

René de Saussure, *Esperanto-II*, Bern 1939

René de Saussure, *Treatises on Word Formation in Esperanto*, published between 1910 and 1919 as monographs.

H. Shenton, *Cosmopolitan Conversation, the Language Problems of International Conferences*, Columbia 1934 (University Press)

Shenton-Sapir-Jespersen, *International Communication*, London 1931 (Kegan Paul)

Shirjaev-Kökeny-Bleier-Kalocsay, *Enciklopedio de Esperanto*, Budapest 1933 (Literatura Mondo)

L. Susan Stebbing, *Thinking to Some Purpose*, London 1941 (Penguin)

P. E. Stojan, *Bibliografio de Internacia Lingvo*, Geneva 1929 (UEA)

Max Talmay, *The problem of an auxiliary international language and its solution*, New York 1923, in *Scientific Monthly*.

Thorndike, *Language Learning*, Columbia 1937 (University Press)

Ernest Weekley, *The English Language*, London 1928 (Ernest Benn)

Eugen Wüster, *Enciklopedia Vortaro Esperanta-Germana*, A-Kor, Leipzig 1923 (Hirt)

Eugen Wüster, *Konturoj de la lingvo-normigo en la tekniko*, Budapest 1936 (*Literatura Mondo*)

L. L. Zamenhof, *Fundamenta krestomatio de la lingvo Esperanto*, Paris 1907, kvina eldono (Hachette)

International Language Library: The reference library of the British Esperanto Association at 36 Penrhyn Road, Kingston-on-Thames, welcomes any serious student of the problem of an I.L. For conditions apply to the Education Secretary, Mr Montague C. Butler.

International Auxiliary Language Association (IALA): Information on its activities may be obtained from its headquarters, 420 Lexington Avenue, New York City, U.S.A.

ESPERANTO: Information and literature on Esperanto may be obtained from The British Esperanto Association, Inc., 140 Holland Park Avenue, London, W.11

IDO: Information and literature may be obtained from The International Language (Ido) Society of Great Britain, 3 Spareleaze Hill, Loughton, Essex.

OCCIDENTAL: Information and literature may be obtained from Britannic Occidental-Association, 23, Womersley Road, London, N.8.

Index